# Life Interrupted

## portraits in a late style

GW00771661

Lateness comes "after something that one has survived."  Theodor Adorno

"Such was my habit, imagining the inner landscapes of others and drawing their portraits—ultimately—from the model I knew best: myself."  Ayad Akthar

# Life Interrupted

## portraits in a late style

### by Judy Schavrien

Copyright ©2021 by Judy Schavrien
All rights reserved. Printed in the United States.

Second edition 2021
First edition 2020

No part of this publication may be reproduced, distributed, or transmitted in any form or by any means, including photocopying, recording, or other electronic or mechanical methods, or by any information storage and retrieval system without the prior written permission of the publisher, except in the case of very brief quotations embodied in critical reviews and certain other noncommercial uses permitted by copyright law.

All art and text is by Judy Schavrien, including the front cover art. Book design is by Judy Schavrien. Acknowledgments for the back cover photograph go to Lozano and Gilbert and for the *Hey, Boomer!* photograph to Elaine Cohen.

LCCN: 2021900030
ISBN-13: 978-0-578-83419-1

JUDY SCHAVRIEN
Walnut Creek, California

www. jesart.net
judys.imagekind.com

Contact: judynow@comcast.net

For **Judith Mayer**, **Abdullah Rahmani,** and the late **David Grene**, whose work on Late Style inspired my own

*Full fathom five thy father lies;*
*Of his bones are coral made;*
*Those are pearls that were his eyes;*
*Nothing of him that doth fade,*
*But doth suffer a sea-change*
*Into something rich and strange.*
*Sea-nymphs hourly ring his knell:*
*Ding-dong.*
*Hark! now I hear them — Ding-dong, bell.*

(Song from I,ii The Tempest)

# PREFACE

## A Pilgrim's Progress

Three days before my fortieth birthday I was mugged. The birthday would arrive on April 4th. I had been working with a mentor to bring about a major change in perspective for that watershed birthday. I wanted a deeper, broader view of life, less focused on my navel. Like most relatively young people, I still had a robust sense of myself as immortal. Then, at minutes from the midnight of April 1st, I was shot in the face. This was an April Fools Day to remember.

The moment of the shooting, and then its aftermath, accomplished two things. It amplified an interest in the human face that I had already possessed. This book, as you will see, contains study after study of the face. The bullet that traveled through my cheek seemed to shatter not just my face but the personality that found its home there. At least I felt as if my personality had fallen into pieces when I "lost face." No face, no person.

The second thing that the shooting did was amplify my need to know the meaning of life, so that I could one day leave the planet without shame or regret. If I knew what death meant, I might catch a glimpse of my assignment in life. I could orient myself and shake off the feeling that I might just be missing the boat. These portraits of mine, "portraits in a Late Style," jibe with the definition of Late Style: Late Style views life in the light of death. The Late Style of Shakespeare, for instance—with Prospero confiding "every third thought shall be my death"— or else of Rembrandt in the final phase of his self-portraits—depicts the mortal fragility of the "bare, forked beast."

As I have aged and distanced from the midnight shooting, the odor, the fragrance of death has receded for some periods. But now, in my 70's, I have lost a number of my closest people. I accompanied one recently in a years-long ordeal of diminishing and finally death; others that I love dearly are living with a terminal diagnosis. A relatively new visitor to my life, to everyone's life, is the COVID-19 virus. This is a catastrophe of much greater girth than the rest, almost too big for the mind to encompass and the heart to take in.

After forty, I studied and practiced for many years with a lama known as a death specialist. The late Sogyal Rinpoche, a Tibetan Buddhist teacher, specialized in what happens between death and rebirth. He was a specialist too in the gaps in this life. Such gaps may be viewed, by analogy with the gap between death and the hereafter, as bardo passages. "Bar" translates from the Tibetan as "in-between" and "do" translates as "suspended" or "thrown." When you are thrown between death and rebirth, or else between one mundane moment, severely interrupted, and the next, this can certainly make for a crisis. It also, however, poses an opportunity. It is a disorientation. This shocked state of mind, which the Tibetans call *hedewa,* is likely, for just that moment, to interrupt bad mental habits, offering an opportunity to widen and deepen, or at the very least refresh, your Awareness.

Buddhism prepares you for the predictable moments, the dying and the death. It can steady you through the unexpected moments as well. It helped me address the shooting that had caught me by surprise. After my forties, I taught to psychology doctoral students the strange and refreshing views in *The Tibetan Book of Living and Dying.* I was also a psychotherapist. How did all this synchronize with my work in the visual arts? During that period, in my forties and onward, I had to reconcile the work of the artist with that of the healer. There would be a danger of my becoming so absorbed in the face of my client that I'd forget to do my actual job. Tracking the movements of the eyes across from me— allowing heart and mind to move with the client's feelings as they reached a crescendo or diminished—this certainly honed my ability to offer at the right time in the right way a healing response. But I could not let my own eyes, the eyes of a painter, neglect the healing task at hand; not, at least, while I was in the process of giving psychotherapy, tending to a client's needs, rather than painting in the studio.

## Portraits in a Late Style/ The Permeable Self

Here, then, is my collection of human creatures. When I am creating these works, I am immersed in the sitter. It is not just a matter of observing the face and the body. I am instead immersed in the face and body as a crystallization of personality and, beyond that, of whatever animates us; I will call that "soul." I immerse in all this fully and directly; not as a cool observer, half there half elsewhere, and not as a devotee of beauty, I mean the kind of beauty that holds you fixated on surfaces. I am often, at the time I am rendering these sitters, quite in love with the people they have grown themselves to be, in love with that process as well, the process of the growing. I am likewise in love with how life has *grown them*, willy-nilly. There has been so much that they did *not* choose. If the painting is of someone I know intimately, then the immersion is doubly true.

Perhaps the most important thread running through my renderings is the following. I would characterize these drawings and paintings as having been done, almost all of them, in a Late Style. What is a Late Style sensibility? It views life in the light of death. It tends to occur in old age but you can discover death, discover it feelingly, at a younger age. You can live in a proximity with death. In other words, Shakespeare's Late Style period, as critics see it, came in his forties and he died in his early fifties.

I will develop both a view of my own Late Style and also of Late Style as critics discern it in the works of others. I do so with two caveats. The first is that some critics dispute whether Late Style—as a style that cuts across historical context—even exists. Is it just a fiction of critics, keeping themselves busy? Late Sophocles, in this ahistorical approach, would share traits with late Shakespeare, late Rembrandt with late Picasso. Is "late" strictly a personal phenomenon in that sense? Can historical and cultural context be ignored by simply lumping these figures together? For the moment, I'll take a pass on that controversy (and address it at another time, in the section called *Tales and Familiars*). The second caveat is that critics assign Late Style almost exclusively to white male geniuses. I'm white; that's all.

There are two major attitudes toward Late Style. They match the iconic theater masks—one smiles and the other frowns. The smiling approach had begun with early critics like Edward Dowden. Dowden characterized Prospero, in *The Tempest*, Shakespeare's last play written solo, as "arrived": serene, wise, in harmony with the cosmos. His arrival may have demanded a certain renunciation, a certain fortitude, but he had indeed arrived. And Prospero could be read as a stand-in for the "late" and accomplished Shakespeare himself.

The second approach comes from critics like Theodor Adorno and his admirer, Edward Said. Emblematic of the approach would be the frowning, not smiling, theater mask. Edward Said, without apology, rejected the dewy-eyed celebration of a late phase. He understood lateness as the Welsh poet Dylan Thomas did in these words to his father: "Do not go gentle into that good night. . . / Rage, Rage against the dying of the light." Adorno celebrated the dissonance of late works by Beethoven; Said celebrated the challenging and abrasive work of Genet, playwright of *The Blacks*. In this second version of Late Style, the creators (and often their creatures) are far from harmonious: they are artists, composers, writers who are in exile,

out of place, out of time. They are "late" enough to declare their views without pleasing others or adhering mindlessly to social myths and conventions. They can hew, in their depictions, to what eye, ear, and heart know: life is not all harmony; it is full of, not just contradictions, but irreconcilables.

The smiling characterization—wise and serene—might appear to apply to the sitter who opens my own particular collection: the painting (ACROSS) is called *Survivor, Judith.* There may be some resignation, but there is fortitude also. This person has been through the mill; she is still here. There is kindliness as well—toward others and even self. It is a post-chemo rendering, so there has clearly been a price to pay. Later in the book, there are drawings of Judith pre-diagnosis, with a curly crown of hair. The hair had been her pride earlier in life: insouciant, she could take all that beauty for granted. But the weathering in Judith as a survivor has accomplished a different kind of beauty.

*The Artist in an Oriental Costume with a Poodle at his Feet*     *Self-portrait with Beret and Turned Up Collar*

"Life in the light of death" reveals that facet of us that is poignant in its fragility. Here today gone tomorrow. My own Late Style often has a dark side, but I do believe it is both alert to the common human dilemma and compassionate. Another characteristic of my style is this: it emphasizes intersecting worlds and a self interrupted. "Life is what happens while you're making other plans." I use an abstract approach to put this across. Not just Judith, but many of my characters are permeable; textures or patterns or whole worlds flow into and through these characters. They are like coelentrates—jellyfish or sea anemones —with currents washing through them. Currents of consciousness, or else currents that are elemental: it could be the light or the swift wind, the slow-growing stone or the bark of a tree. These elements texture the character. In the case of Judith, in the portrait called *Survivor, Judith*, light not only shines through her but also comes from within. It lights up, all at once, both herself and what she sees.

Perhaps Judith is in a weather-worn state, but she is also, somehow, arrived. The fanfare might be less clarion than the fanfare, as Dowden would have it, for Prospero. But at the very least, Judith is present and accounted for. Flesh and blood, heart and soul, she has become, as anyone versed in a bit of Yiddish would call her, "a mensch," someone who is right there for you.

**Both the Smile and the Frown**

In the early Rembrandt above, light shines from without and illumines, with splendid metallic glints, the young man's fancy dress and cheeky exterior. He has accoutrements— his poodle, his fine, even phallic, feather. By contrast, the late self-portrait reveals Rembrandt in essence — lit from within, weathered and worn perhaps, but concentrated in those sharp, seeing eyes. True, there is a good deal of sadness in the eyes and crenellated brow, but there is irony as well, a sharpened wit. It is there in the uptick at the eybrow. Finally, there is compassion. To characterize the late Rembrandt self-portrait, I would make a cocktail mix of the smiling and frowning approach to Late Style. There is enough acceptance, despite life's contradictions, that the painter, as he is depicted, can focus on the task at hand, his self-portrait in the making. And, in place of the young man's glamorous self-display, there is complexity and richness in the look, a penetrating and humane discernment. In that sense, there is loveliness.

What if you have lived through the fall, like the fall of a giant oak, felling not just the splendid personality you have fashioned, taking such pains to do so through the years, but the whole world with it? As the great psychologist William James suddenly realized for himself—we all die, and therefore we are all in some sense failures. The failure of the "personality project," I might call it, that is also a kind of death. There's many a young soldier, upholding his or her honor, who would rather suffer the first kind of death, which is literal death, than the death that is dishonor and failure. The old Rembrandt, at least the figure in the late self-portrait, has seen failure. (The actual Rembrandt had seen many: including loss of dear ones; bankruptcy; his fall from preeminence as a new era ushered in a thin, slick style of painting to replace his thick one). Many of my characters, because they have reached a late phase in their lives, come to see others and themselves more candidly. They would (and did) consent to being depicted warts and all. Warts and all is the Rembrandt in the late portrait, and he is splendid. In short, I aspire to be that kind of artist, with a penchant for candor, inviting an intimacy. The works needn't show too much polish—if they did, they'd require less investment by the viewer to enter into the character's world, using her own insides to fill in the gaps. Less polish, if done right, can draw the willing viewer in close.

There is an autobiographical moment I have neglected to mention; and it is relevant to the discussion of the "smiling" brand of Late Style, the one that highlights a certain reconciliation with the ways of the cosmos. The moment tracks back to my having been mugged and shot, and, before that, to my work with a mentor. She was a psychic, one that police sometimes used, and used successfully, to get a new angle on a crime that was stumping them. In the course of my work with her, and leading up to the shooting, I had landmark dreams in which I was shot and yet survived the incident. The dreams assured me —I would survive. Of course I had no notion whatsoever that these dreams were literal and that such a shooting was waiting in the wings. When it *did* occur, the wonders of consciousness opened up to me. Consciousness could *foresee*; it could outwit Newtonian Time. On the other hand, the horrors of the world opened up as well. I had years in front of me, traveling the world, in which I attempted to put the two halves of my perceiving self together. Body workers would look at me, astounded by what their hands were telling them. —"You are two different people . . . on the right side dark and on the left side bright . . ." I was eventually able to conclude that this world of ours is both terrible and wondrous; it is not a case of either/or. After years of globetrotting, although I was newly undertaking study with the Tibetan Buddhists, I could also find my answers in the words of a man from my own tribe, Rabbi Heschel. He approached the mystery of living first and foremost by way of an always fresh vision, by way of awe. Awe was his religion. I could make it mine as well.

### Imagination as a True Faculty

In the *Survivor, Judith* portrait on a previous page, Judith may be "almosting" a new world, almost catching a glimpse of it, almost coming to live in it. There she is in a light-drenched world, different from the world of mundane joys and disappointments. She may have had a glad glimpse of such a world, one that eliminates the separation between feet and the ground they walk on, eyes and the light they see. The vision is there in the *Tempest* song that introduces the *Preface.* "Nothing of him that doth fade,/But doth suffer a sea-change/ Into something rich and strange." This song is an imagining of the return to nature after death; it is an imagining shot through with awe. "[O]f his bones are coral made" is a far cry from "dust to dust." Can it be said "objectively" that there is no such sea-change awaiting human beings, no Utopia on earth and no Heaven to come? So many of us do believe in Utopia, whether we admit it or not. The great success of the song sung by John Lennon, *Imagine,* indicates a common human longing. In fact the vision of the song—no laws, no possessions, living life in peace—practically quotes a speech in Shakespeare's *The Tempest.* It is spoken by Gonzalo, a decent old fellow who, having landed by mishap on a New World island, like the ones discussed in 16th century Europe and England in feverish tones, sings the praises of the Utopia he would create if he ruled this new island. Even if it is never to be had, the fantasy of such a place, and such a way of being, is undying and ever-motivating.

Likewise we believe in and have experienced Hell on earth. The imaginative faculty not only colors but also shapes our experience. It is not a trivial faculty, as in "mere fantasy," but a true one. It makes for the hauntings, the night terrors, as well as the dreams of peace on earth. The new world might be a Hell of sorts, a sudden shocking glimpse of Death's country brought on by a terminal diagnosis (cf. *Judith, Post-Chemo*, ACROSS) or else it might well be the Heaven of a light-drenched world.

My portraits cultivate the inner, the inward. They are about more than personality as it permeates the

face, the posture, the body as a whole. Instead a light falls on something one might call soul—whatever looks out at you, alive, seeming to have its own history and destiny. This soulful vitality has, of course, its own immediacy as well. Often, when the work is in color, a certain music expresses itself in, around, and through the coloring. There are rhythms binding even what seems disparate and conflicting in a face and in a life. I would say that about my painting (BELOW) called *Survivor*. There is music in the rhythms set by the vertical strokes of the pattern; and there is an overall music as well, carried by the various lines and strokes and prevailing colors. If there are worlds that intersect, background and foreground, they find their confluence.

Where the inner world meets the outer, disruption and a reconciling unity can happen all at once.

I have taken the liberty to set my work in a philosophical context rather than sticking strictly with an autobiographical or visual one. Why? Because the later it is, the more I feel licensed, even driven, to say what I really want to say. For those who are skeptical of my interpretations, or prefer images with minimal noise around them, I am fine, at least for the purposes of the art gathered here, if these words are passed over. The artist is no ultimate authority; she is a commentator with some insider knowledge. The visuals, after all, are entitled to their own life. For those who enjoy commentary on the images, I am glad for your company in this my *essaie*, my explorative attempt. In all cases, whether you be word or image lover or both, may the portraits that follow engage your interest and your heart.

## A NOTE ON PROCESS

For many pieces presented here, I worked from live models, drawing and painting on the iPad. For others I used ink, charcoal, and/or pastel on paper. The third portion were completed not just with mixed media but with a mixed modal approach, shuttling between hand and digital process. If you are curious, please check the *List of Works* at the back of this book. There you will find the title, year of production, size, and medium as they correspond to the numbered images.

# ACKNOWLEDGMENTS

My thanks go, first and foremost, to my best friend Judith Mayer, utterly dear to my heart and my very best subject for a portrait. The way she meets her life's challenges and helps others to meet theirs is an ongoing inspiration to me. Furthermore she keeps me laughing; and that is a priceless gift.

I also owe a debt of gratitude to those who model as either a day job or a vocation. Their generosity and skill has often amazed me. Likewise great gratitude to artist Jody Mattison, for her canny setups and lightings in the live figure sessions, for her diligent and deft mentoring, and for the extraordinary being that she is, embracing and instructing people of all kinds on all levels.

Next I thank my good friends and colleagues who reviewed the manuscript, including Carol Osmer, Elaine Cohen, Frances Kalfus, Valentine McKay-Riddell, Richard Woodrow, Judith Mayer, Cecelia Wambach, Bonnie Davenport, and the late and dear Geoffrey Luebbert. I am also grateful to Bonnie for helping, as my Focusing partner, to keep me sane through the production of this book—and through the years.

I give a special thanks to the non-profit organization R.E.A.L. (Refugee Education and Learning International) for including me, as Artist-in-Residence, in their ministry on Lesvos. During that month on the Greek island, in July of 2019, I was able to offer some help to refugees and to discover, at the same time, some unexpected healing for myself. Cecelia Wambach, co-founder and former president, was instrumental in that. I selected a few of the pieces I did there for inclusion in this volume. One of the refugees whose portrait appears in this book, Abdullah Rahmani, proved ultimately to be an art colleague of mine and, even more important, a soulmate. We have kept each other afloat through the dark times.

Last, but far from least, I gladly acknowledge my debt to two mentors and friends. The first is the late Harold Rosenberg, art critic for *The New Yorker*. The second is the late David Grene. I thank him for his astonishingly direct and candid work in *Reality and the Heroic Pattern: Last Plays of Ibsen, Shakespeare, and Sophocles*. I must also acknowledge, with great gratitude, the work of Gerald McMullan, in his several books, but especially in the volume edited by him and Sam Smiles, *Late Style and its Discontents*; their own essays and those of the commentators they enlisted greatly advanced not only my thinking on the subject but also my hearing and seeing.

# TABLE OF CONTENTS

# CROSSCURRENTS

1.  **Survivor, Judith**

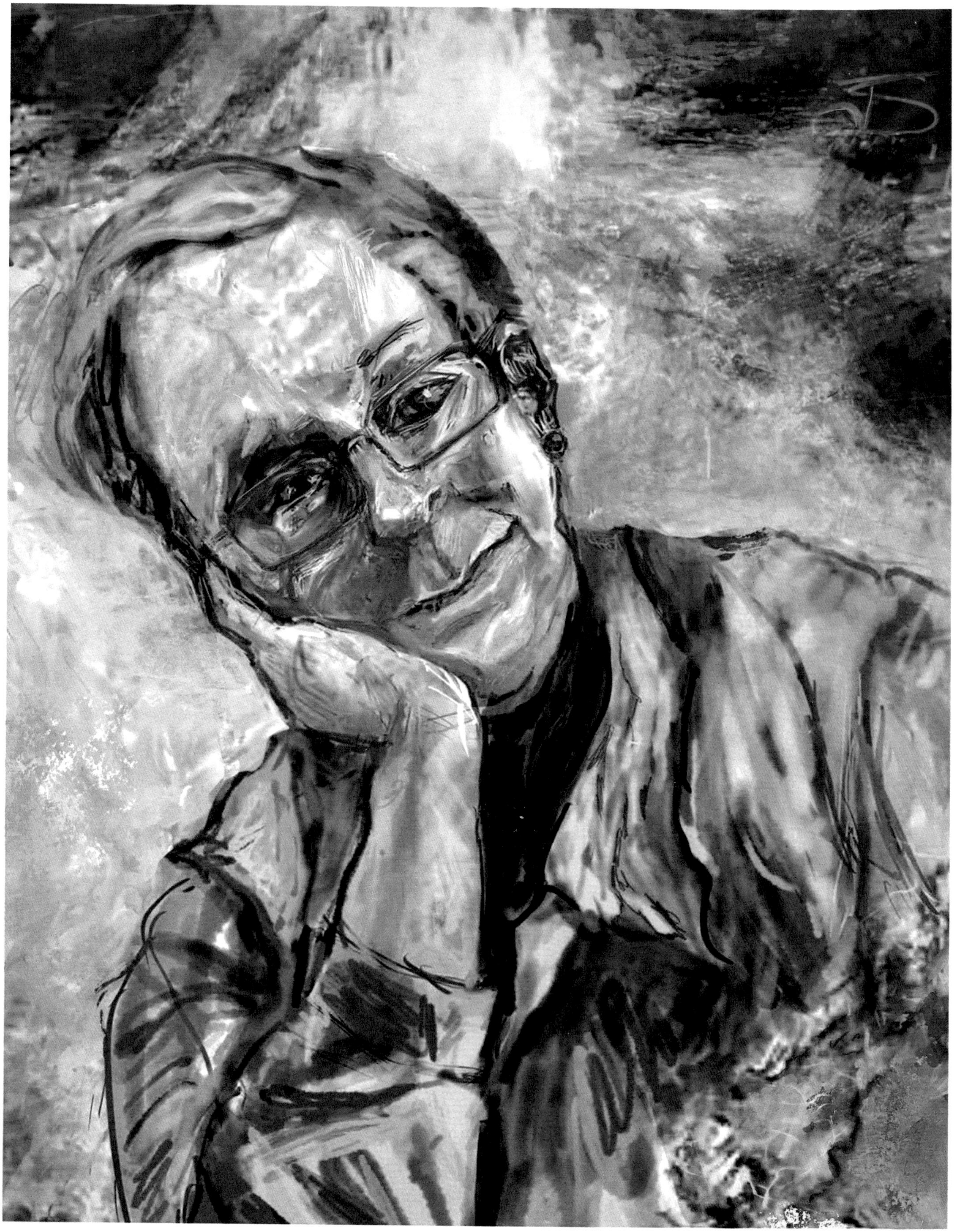

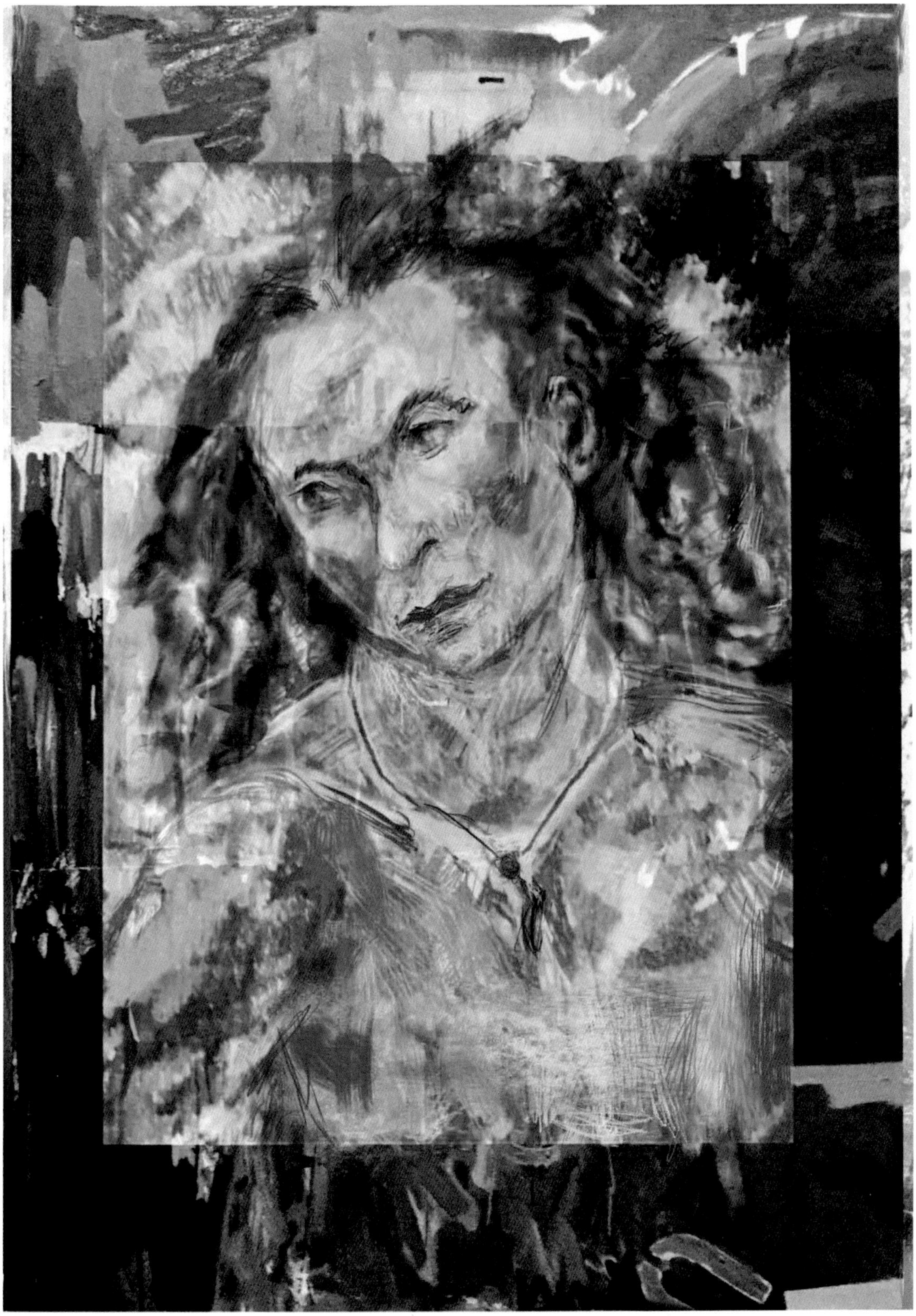

2., 3. **Brian in Dreadlocks** and **Brian in Dreadlocks II**

Some have looked at these two works and said "archangel" (elemental lights and winds, flying hair). This is the model Brian, a most unusual type, with a personality all his own. He loves bulldogs, with an expert's knowledge, is a devoted and deeply curious chef, traveling to learn recipes. He is chatty, quite funny with his gently mocking human commentary. He has sculpted his lean body to a near perfection,

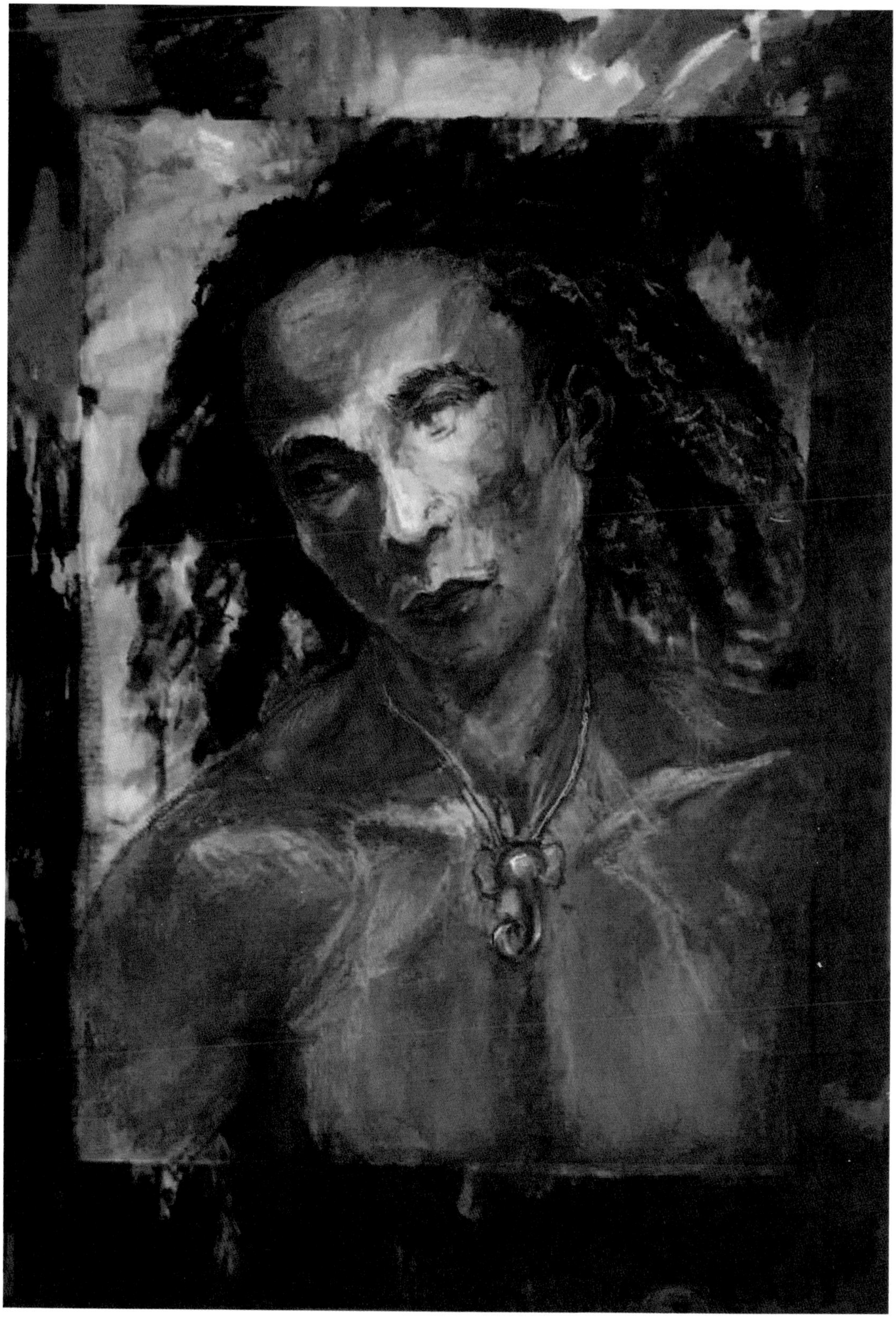

but I guess that he is somewhat haunted. I infer this as he jerks himself out of the chair to take a break. It is as if he moves some resistant part of himself —the other Brian—by sheer will. You cannot help but love him, what with his discipline, his chatty presence, and his mahogany beauty, accented by the Chocktaw cheekbones of a mixed heritage. But you acknowledge that you hardly know him . . . and would never, unless admitted to a very privileged inner circle.

## 4.  Life like leaves falling

In this painting a woman is textured by a texturing cosmos. There is, to my mind, a wistfulness about her. She reaches out but there is a *something* beyond her grasp. She marinates in color, a moody teal and turquoise. Compounds are separating; there is a scattering like leaves in a season with soft winds. She endures nature's decomposing of her. There does remain a desire to be fulfilled, which just manages to hold her together. There is a would-be agency in the arm that reaches out and in the large-enough but lax hand.

   Texture texture texture.  Only gradually has the texturing and patterning of the world, of the cosmos, everywhere, compelled my attention. It asks to be comprehended feelingly— with senses and mind and heart. I find myself, and others who age along with me, not only cognizant of the textures, but increasingly dominated by them. There are the patterns— birth, youth, old age, death, joy and suffering, rebirths of a sort, the predictable and the unpredictable. Was this happening when I was young? Did I fail to notice?

   Returning to the teal blue patch in this painting, with its turquoise lights, the saturated sea-change beauty of it. Perhaps it counterbalances the wistful look, wistful outstretch of the gesture. Color is music. It is a gratuitous gift from the heart of creation, a generosity at the Source.

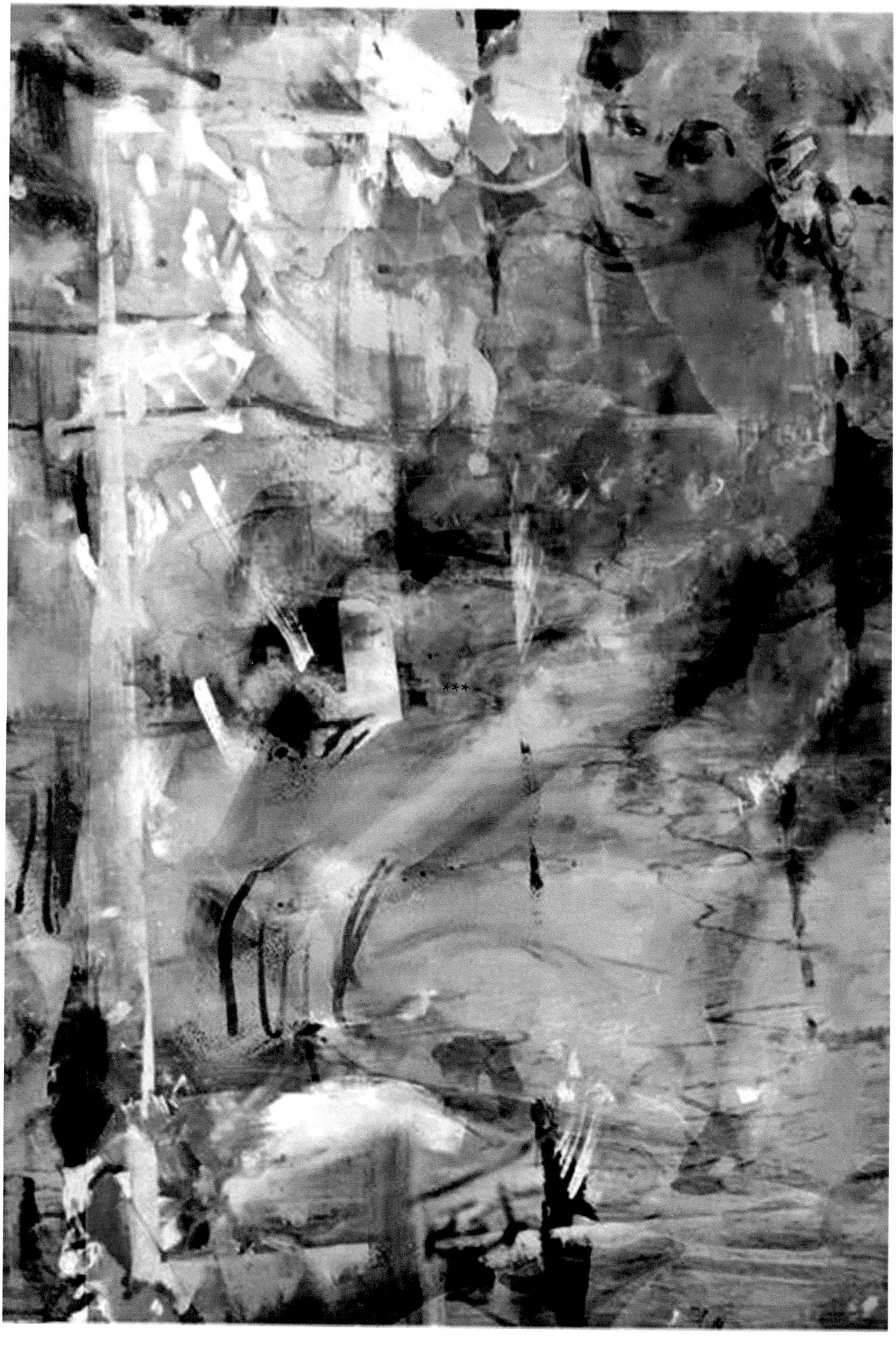

## 5. The Witness

As to the model for this image, I cannot tell you about him, because the image sprang from my head. I *can* say that the live and feelingful ruminations of the subject in the painting are oddly juxtaposed with his seeming to be carved from stone. On the other hand, he would not be suitable for the mummy case of a pharoah, depicting the deathless ruler *sub specie aeternitatis*. What is depicted instead is a person glimpsed in a private moment; the painting is a freezeframe of a soul in progress, one with a history. So much has been attempted and endured. Life has carved itself in his flesh as time carves itself into stone or, then again, into the surface of bark.

Like many of my figures, *The Witness* displays an asymmetry in his face. He bears, at least as I see him, a public side and then again a more private side—bluer, brooding.

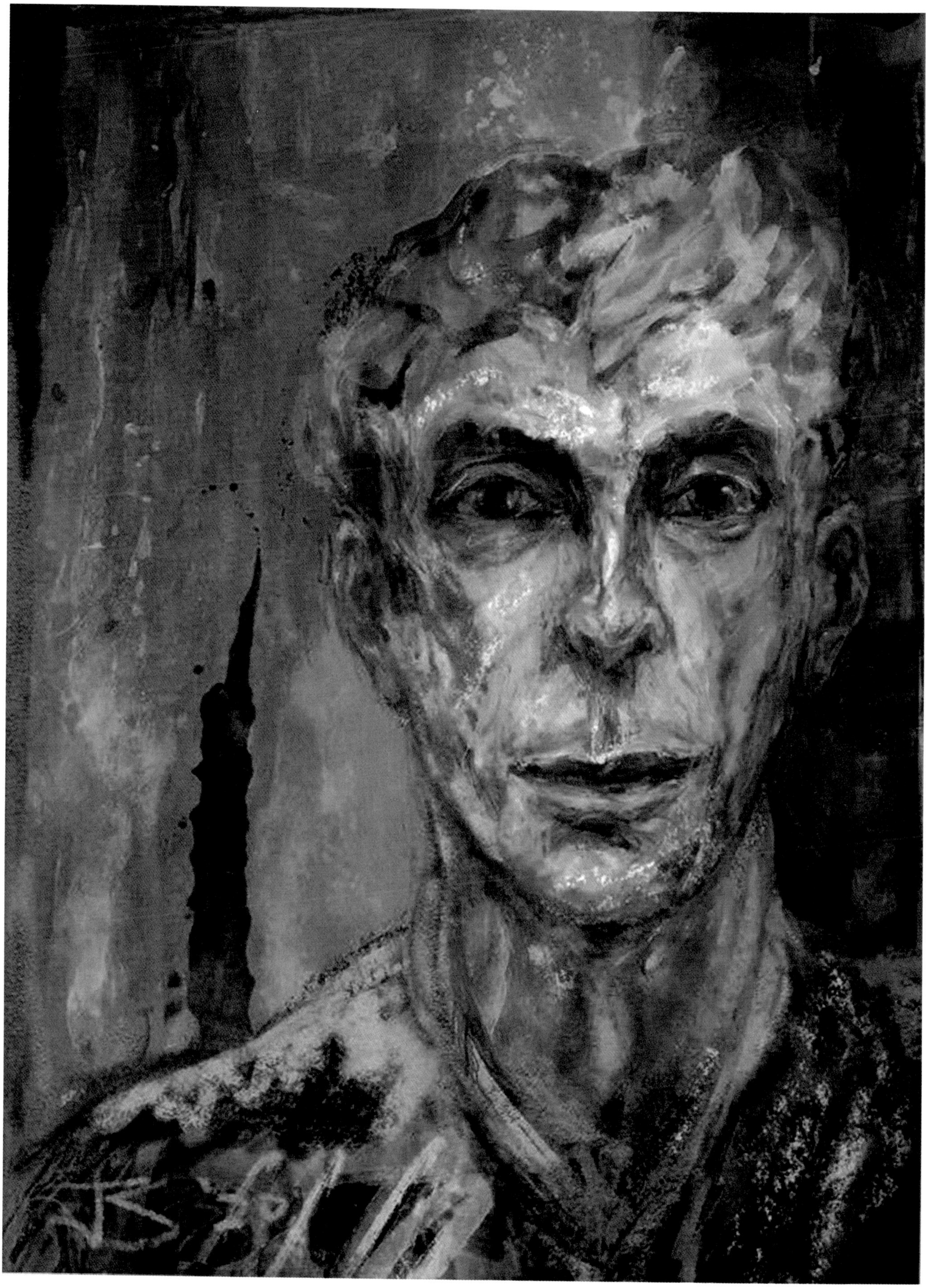

## 6. Self-Portrait at Lesvos

During the summer of 2019, I was an Artist-in-Residence for the non-profit organization *Refugee Learning and Education International*. Above is a self-portrait I painted while watching so much human tragedy play out among the refugees on the island of Lesvos in Greece. The massive inflows from 2015 onward were cramming the tents of refugee camps like Moria. It was an agony and a privilege to witness people of many ethnicities—Syrians, Afghans, Iraqis, Ethiopians, Somalis, and more—take on the challenges of cohabiting peaceably, though crammed together, and of simply enduring in pursuit of a livable life.

In September of 2020, one-third of Moria burned down. The immediate cause was unclear; nevertheless, it was a camp built for 3000 people in tents which came to hold 20,000, and new COVID restrictions may well have put the match to the tinderbox.

## 7. The Refugee

In a world of threatening currents, he is still in flight.

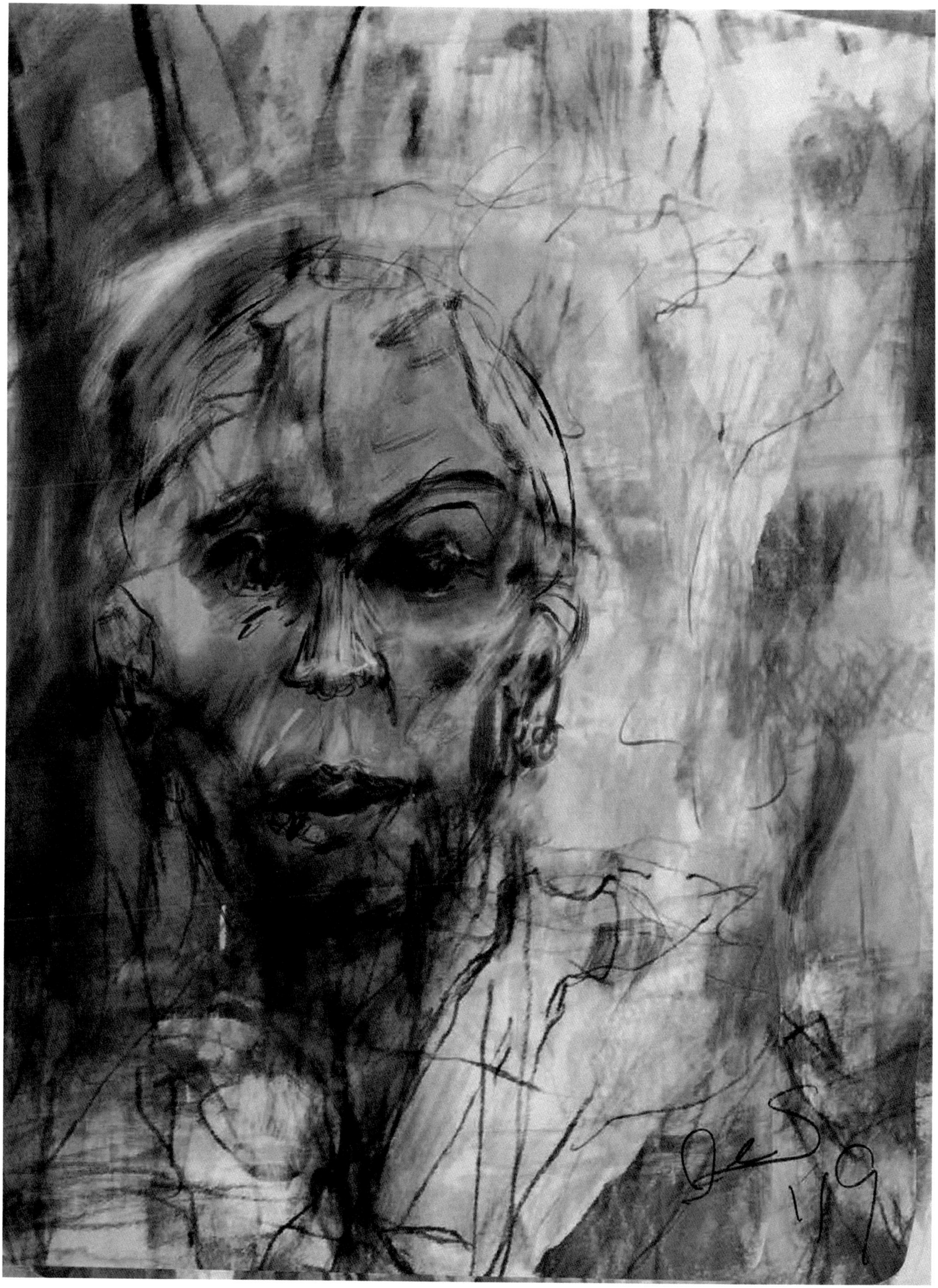

## 8. **Grandmother Hope**

The style here is not realistic exactly but neither is it cartooning. There is perhaps something childlike in the approach, or something mythifying. Clearly there is a narrative in this woman's face. In fact, there really *is* a narrative, in real life, that belongs to this woman. She is a Syrian grandma who saved six children. I drew her from a photo taken by a friend who was present when, after a more-than-perilous sea journey, the woman landed as a refugee on the shores of Lesvos. She had bundled up her neighbors' children, their mothers dead from the war, and carried them along on her escape.

At this moment she is relieved to have made a success of this dangerous enterprise. She is nevertheless apprehensive, as she confided to my friend, that the Greek government will carry off the children.

The blobs in the background of my portrayal, along with the lightning jags, might allude to the war scenes left behind. At the least, it all belongs to her inner world, with its lingering memories. If she is dignified and at peace, it is peace in the eye of the storm.

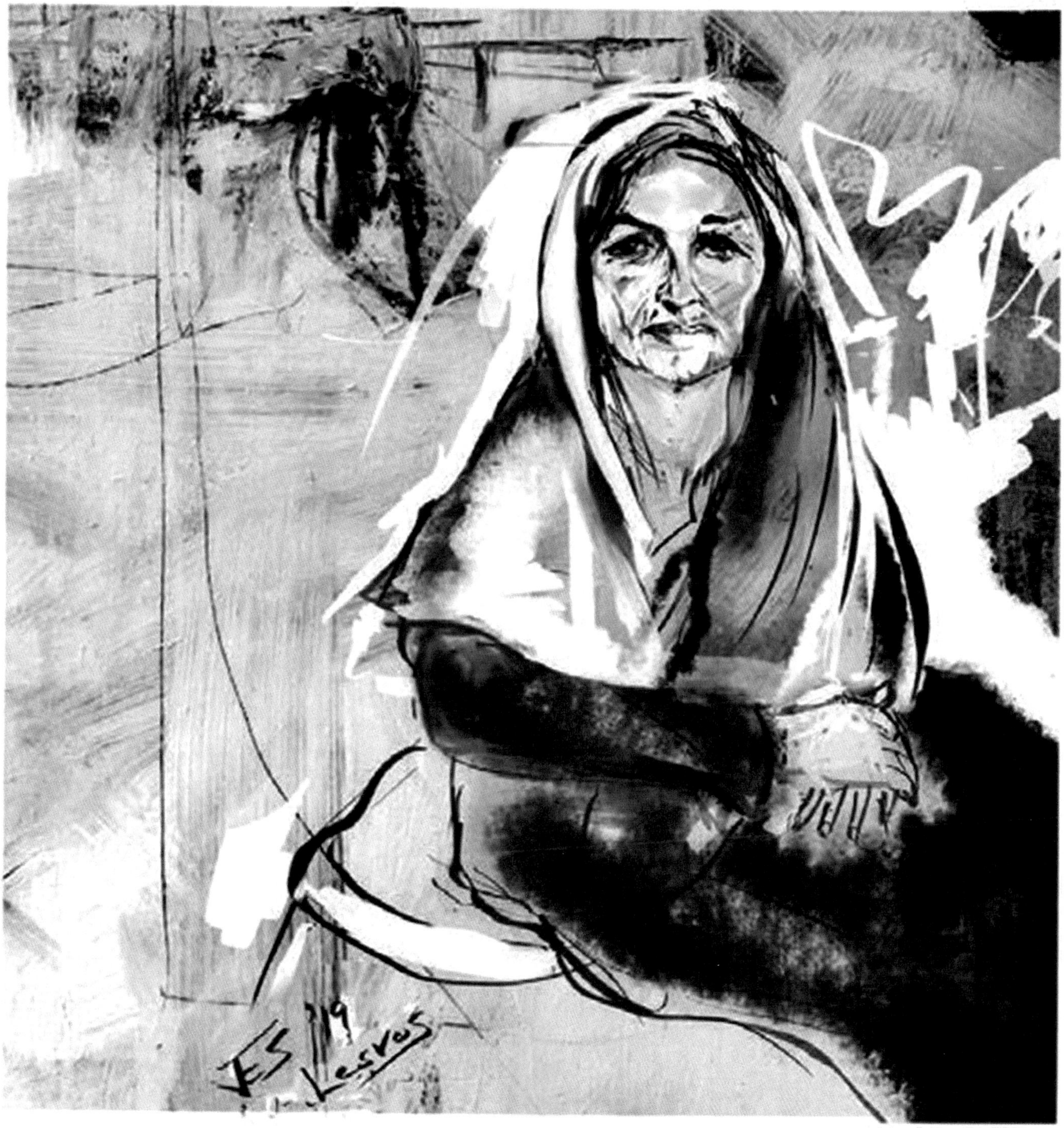
JES '19
Lesvos

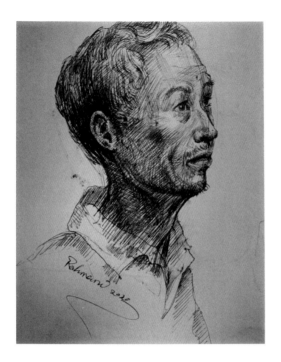 

Abdullah did **Old Man** and **Crows** during his ongoing flight as a refugee, when he lacked access to paints; but he drew and drew.

## 9. **Abdullah**

This is Abdullah Rahmani. I met him at the art center on Lesvos run by *The Hope Project*. We became dear friends. He is a young painter from the Hazara tribe, a tribe persecuted by the Pashtuns who populate the Taliban and dominate Afghanistan. They take particular objection to Abdullah because he paints images of people and animals; in a strict Islamic interpretation, this offends the one Allah whose provenance is souls. Visuals should steer clear of these soul-like images.

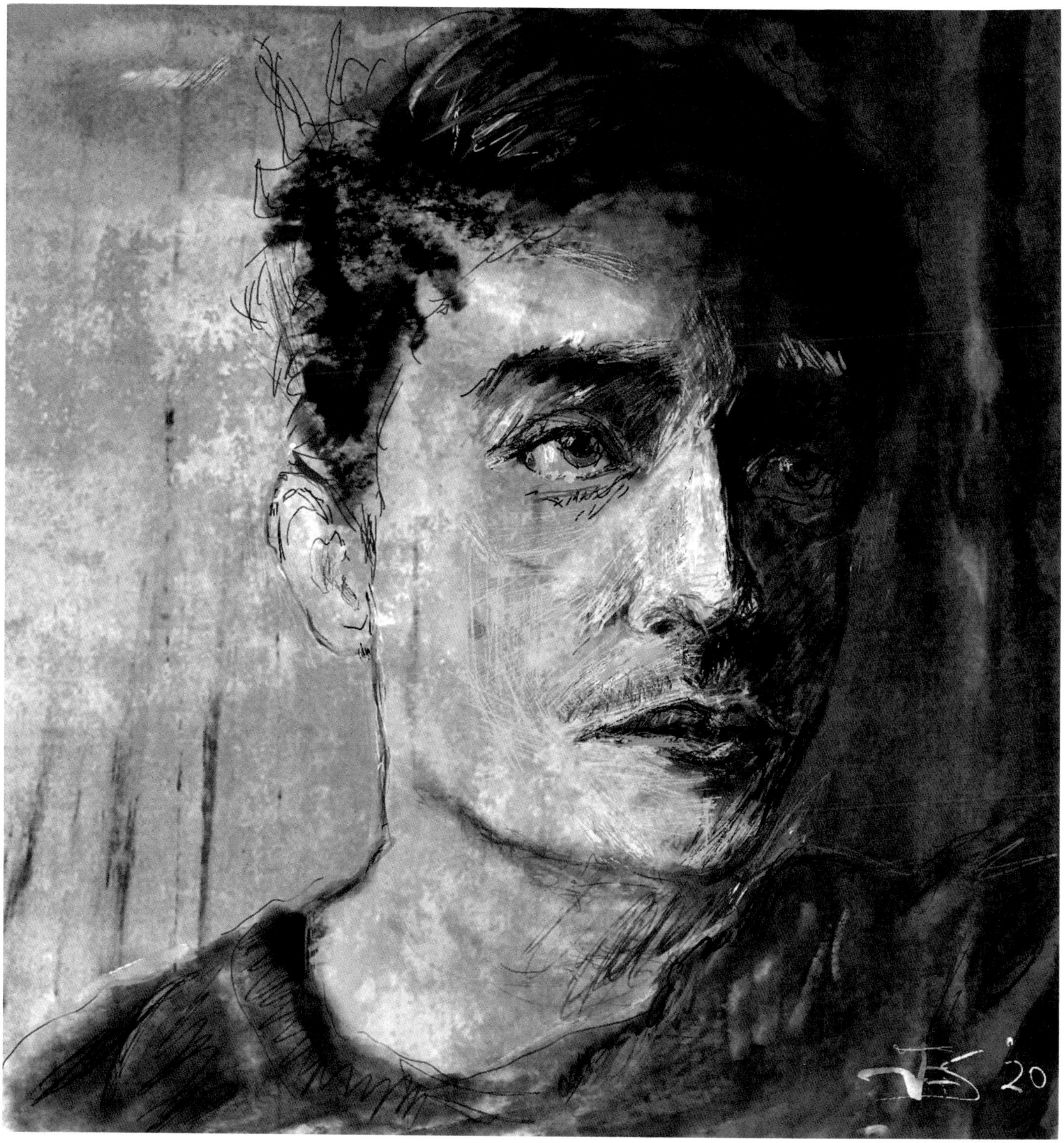

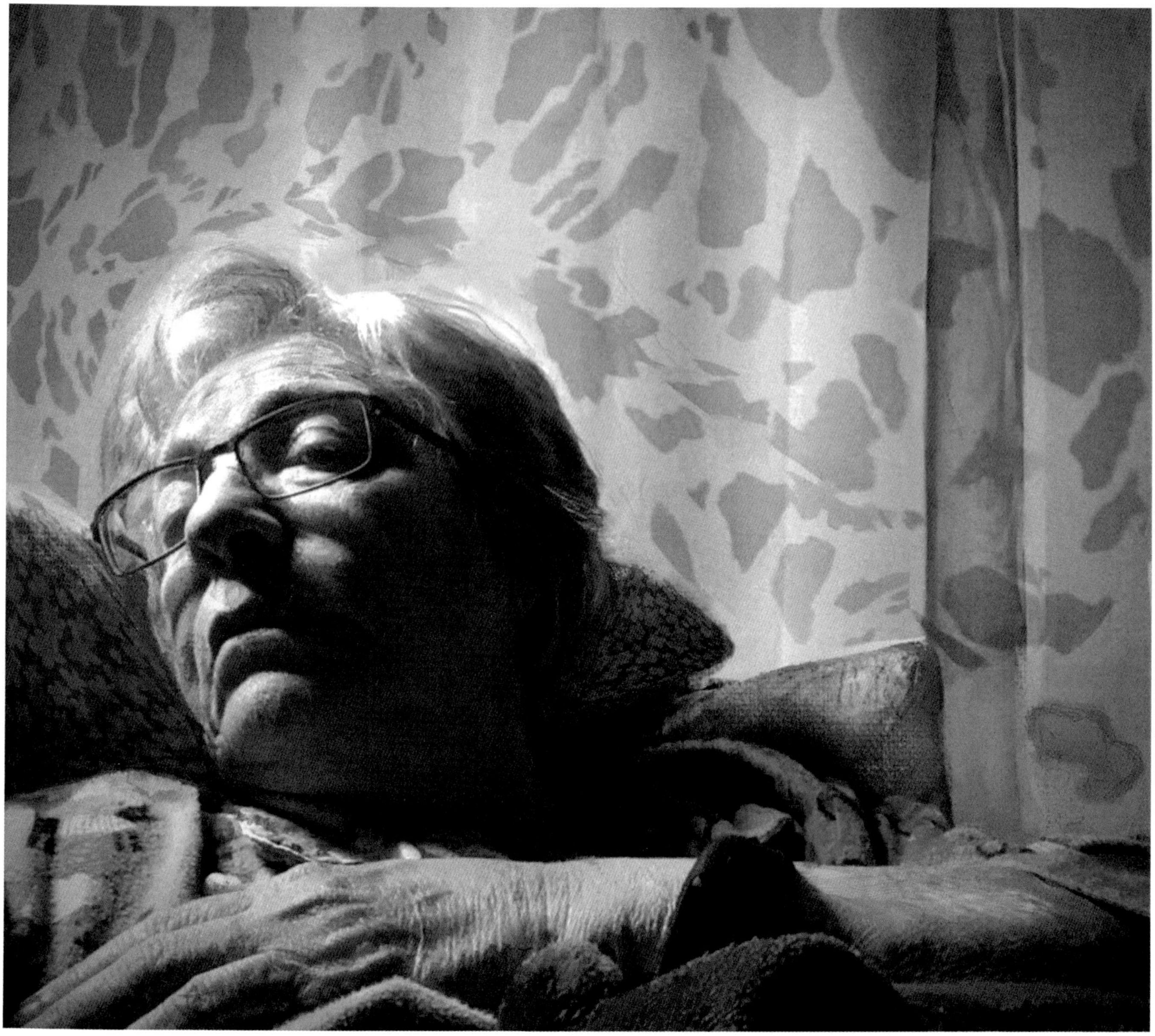

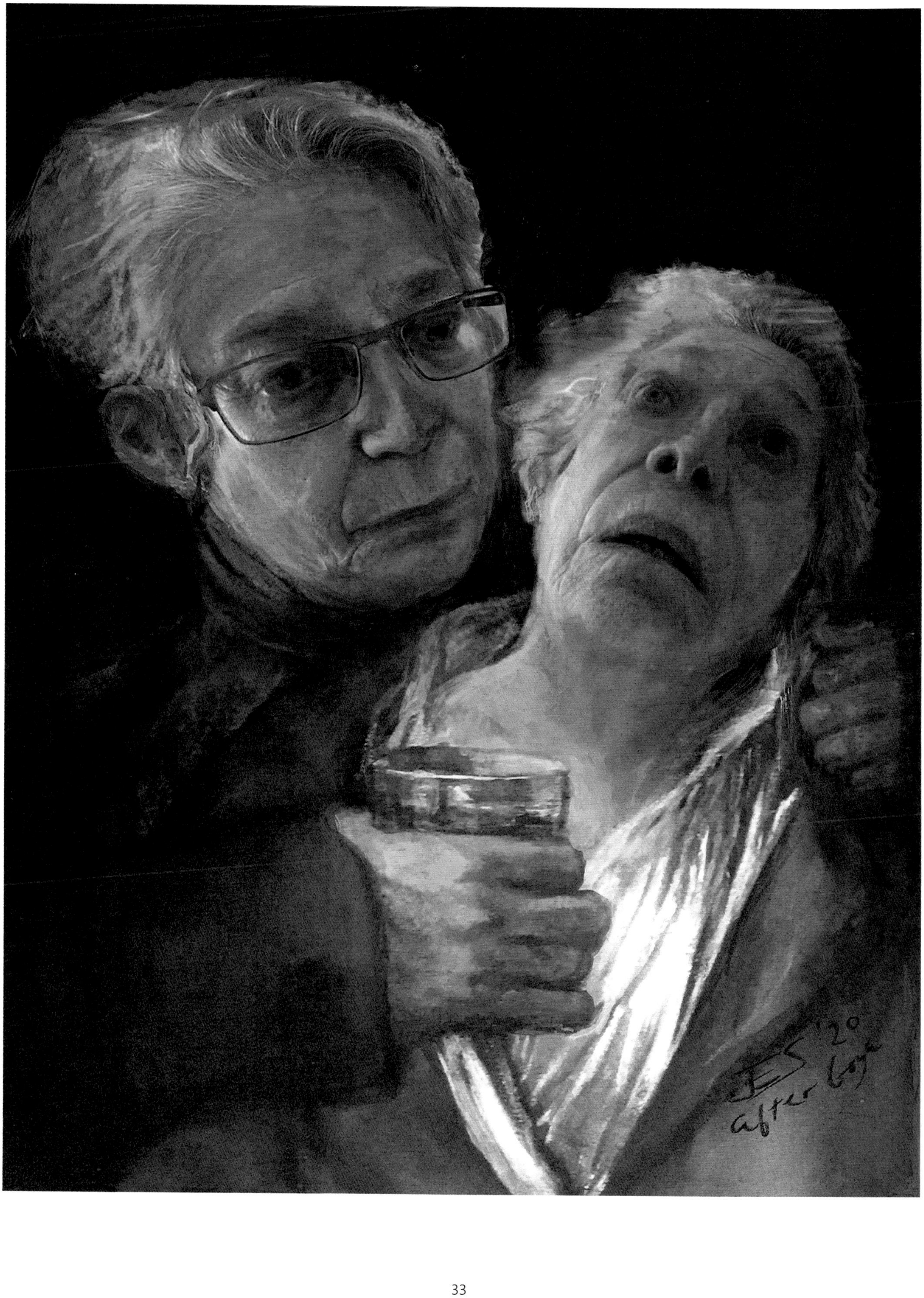
after Goya

## 10.  A Certain Melancholy (Sheltering-in-Place)

I have noticed, regarding recent generations of photo realistic painters, that a good deal of their visual talent gets deployed in "the setup." They are almost film directors. A setup. Then they take the shot. Then they paint. This bears on my own experimentation in this painting. I believe the outcome betrays me as an art film enthusiast.

For the rest, as always, I try to work with a certain candor. Granted, that the mood, the look, is sad and somewhat fixed; it's one of the many places a person can go—especially when that locked down, locked in feeling has an "objective correlative," an outside world to match the inner. Locked down, locked in—it was a fact—that's what we were.

## 11.  Caring in a Time of Plague

In the previous two paintings, I depart from interpenetrating layers. Still, I include the works in this section on crosscurrents because they fit, as compassion narratives, with the refugee paintings. These are all interrupted lives.

*Caring in a Time of Plague* (p.33) was done in the era of COVID-19, as was *A Certain Melancholy* (p.32). I was one of the many who sheltered in place alone. So the only live model I could access was myself. In *Caring*, however, the face of the person who is so very ill, though copied from my own face, took its inspiration from a friend who had just gone through a long ordeal of dying. The painful thinness, due in part to the cancer wasting syndrome, reduced my friend's face to a vision reminiscent of Auschwitz—as both of us, in our Jewishness, were well aware. There is the black space in the mouth, prescient of the gape right before death, when a person, at the brink, still gasps for that final breath. These images, what I'd seen as I watched my friend, had haunted me, and COVID-19 seemed the right moment to transfer them from my inner eye and grieving heart to the paper.

The painting also took its inspiration from one done by Goya in 1820. Critics like Robert Hughes speculated that the patient in the painting may have been suffering from the "Eastern plague." Goya's *Self-Portrait with Dr. Arrieta* portrayed Arrieta nursing the painter back from the brink.

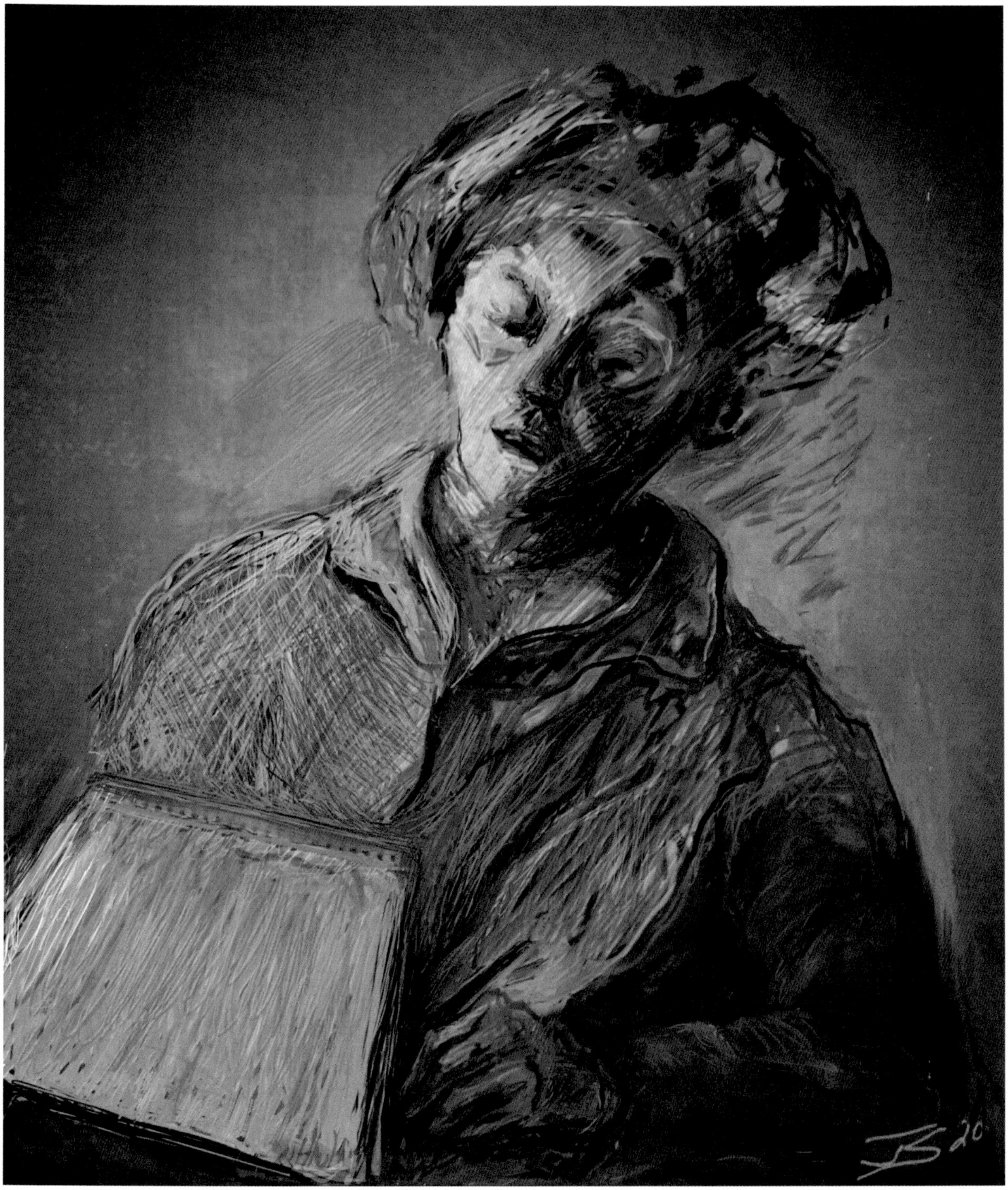

12. **The Artist in Beret and Pajamas**

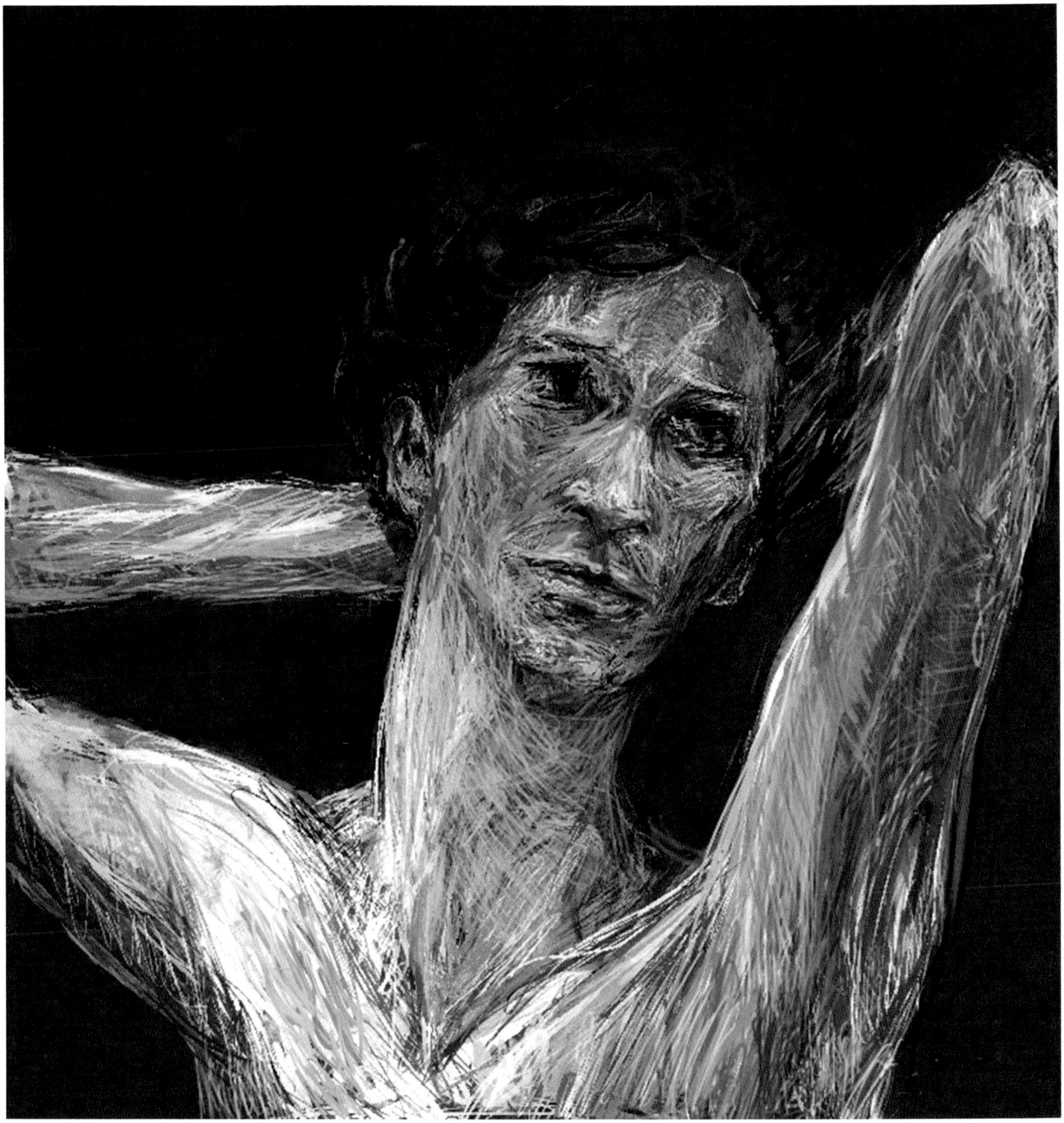

13. **The Longing**

## 14. **Reflections**

A friend of mine remarked: "It's as if the statue of liberty stepped down and stripped for a wine break." Yes, she has broad shoulders, but, like many of us, especially old people and artists, she carries her experience solo. There is a dark brooding; perhaps the performing of a kind of life review. This is endemic to late-in-life, and therefore turns up frequently in Late Style. Another friend, an artist colleague, enjoyed "the life lines in the sketch. You're actually drawing living-ness in the skin and body. The stroke and the color are very veinlike, very blue blooded, very movement oriented, almost like soothing the being with your brush."

I did this digital painting during the COVID shelter-in-place. Perhaps the woman in the painting is sheltering-in as well. She does seem to have a comfort in her body; there has been some coming to terms. The chiaroscuro play of light and shadow on her naked face and limbs helps to create, I would suggest, a bardo moment. She is "thrown in-between."

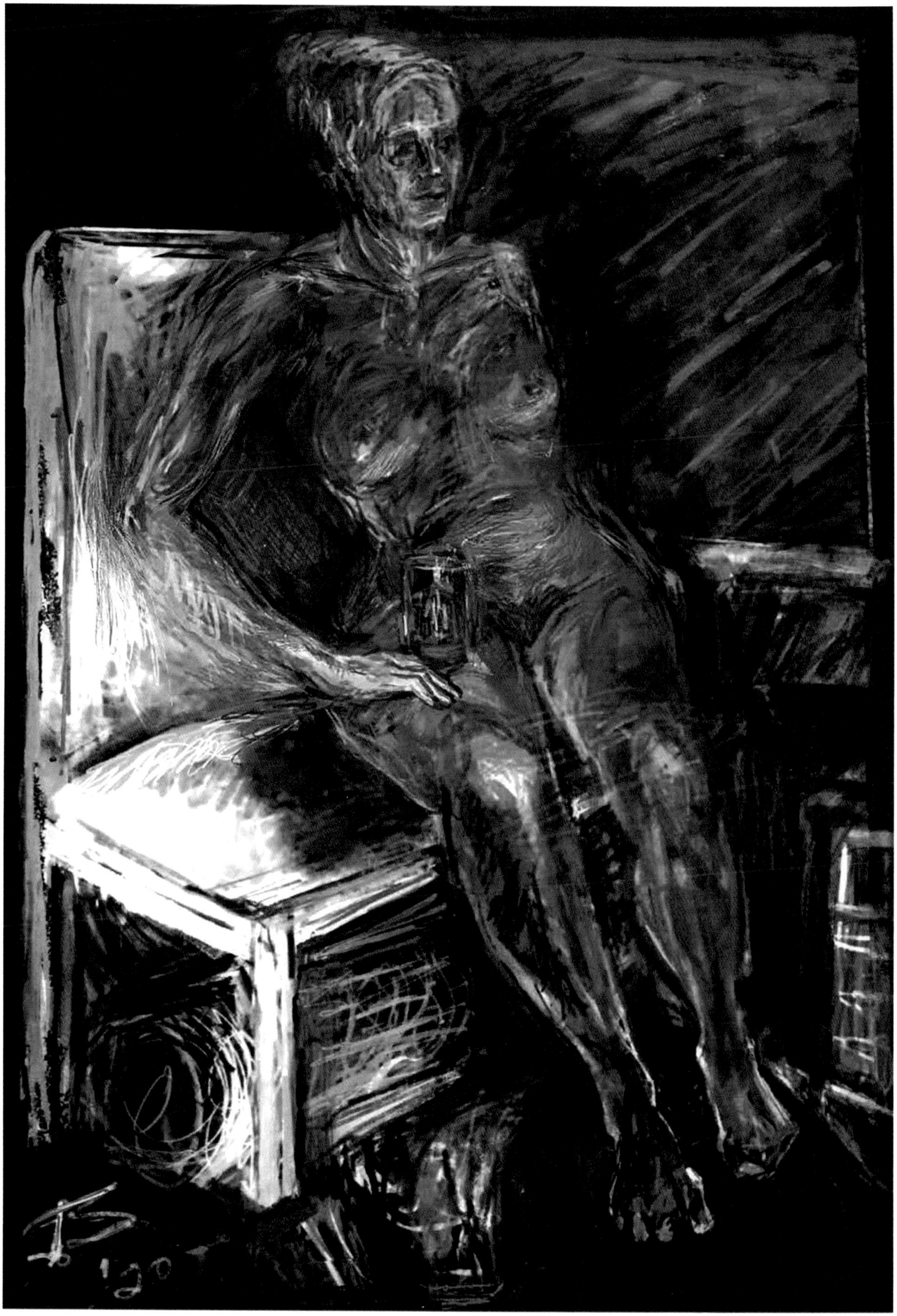

### 15. **Torch Singer**

Seal is a singer I first heard at Joni Mitchell's 75th birthday concert. He turned *Both Sides Now* into a torch song—tore your heart out and sprang flowers from it all at once. I noticed scars on his face and later learned that he has a kind of blood disease that causes them. Sometimes you hear something that makes your jaw drop—those raspy renderings. What Satchmo did on the up side, he was doing with Mitchell's sophisticated blues.

In this piece, done on the iPad, I used my favorite pthalo and turquoise, plus a red not altogether pleasant, to express a hard-lived life and a hard-won authority. I set the singer in a vertical scroll rather than a rectangle, living at a jazzy slant.

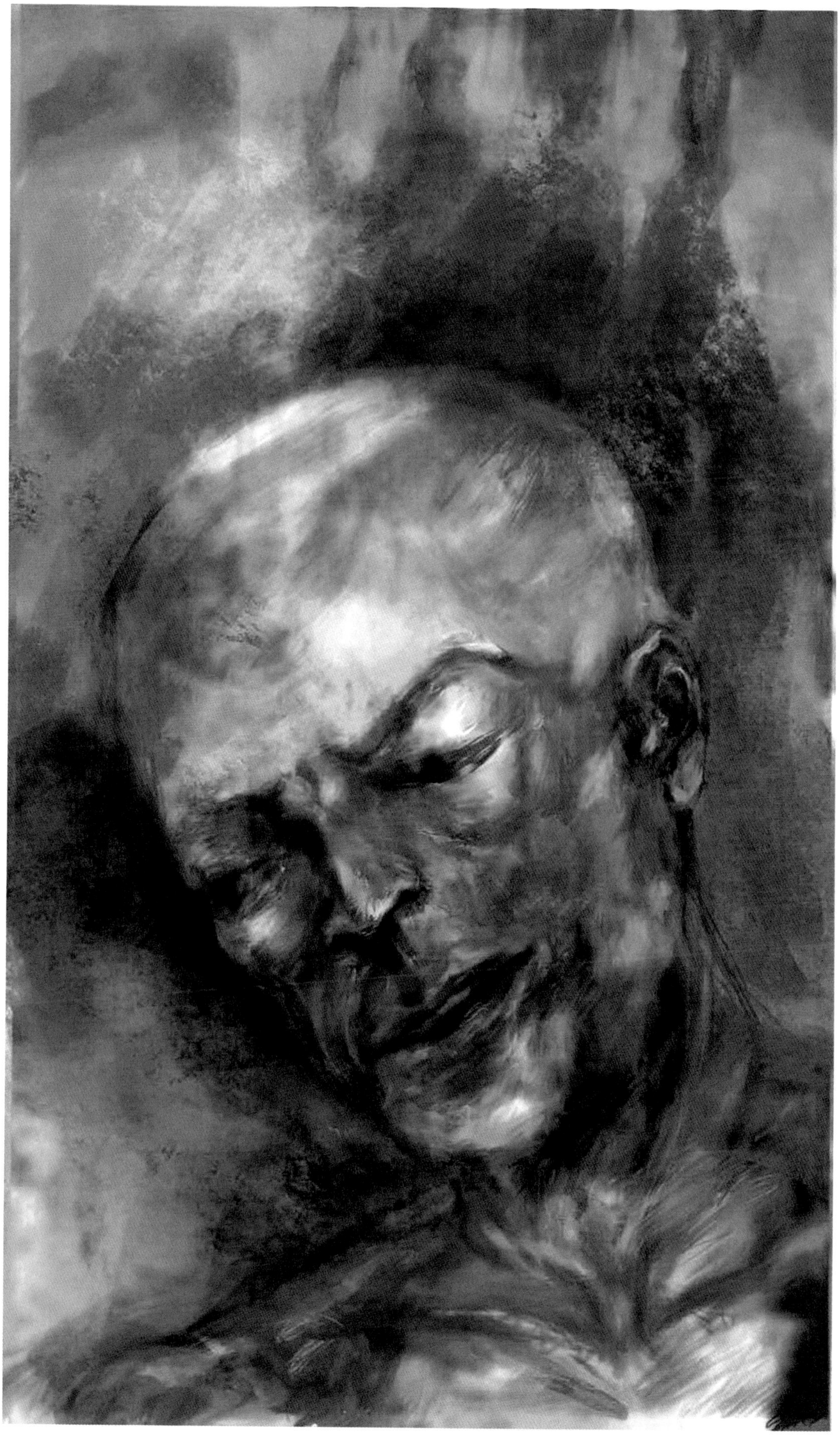

### 16. Judith, Post-Chemo

This is yet another take on Judith. The hat, lovely in its colors, contrasts with a certain austerity in Judith's face and expression. I began this painting in pastel, then did another round on it with the iPad. More rounds with each medium, of course, but I chose finally an early version because, as I kept working, I had unwittingly lost the look in the eyes—and the look was paramount.

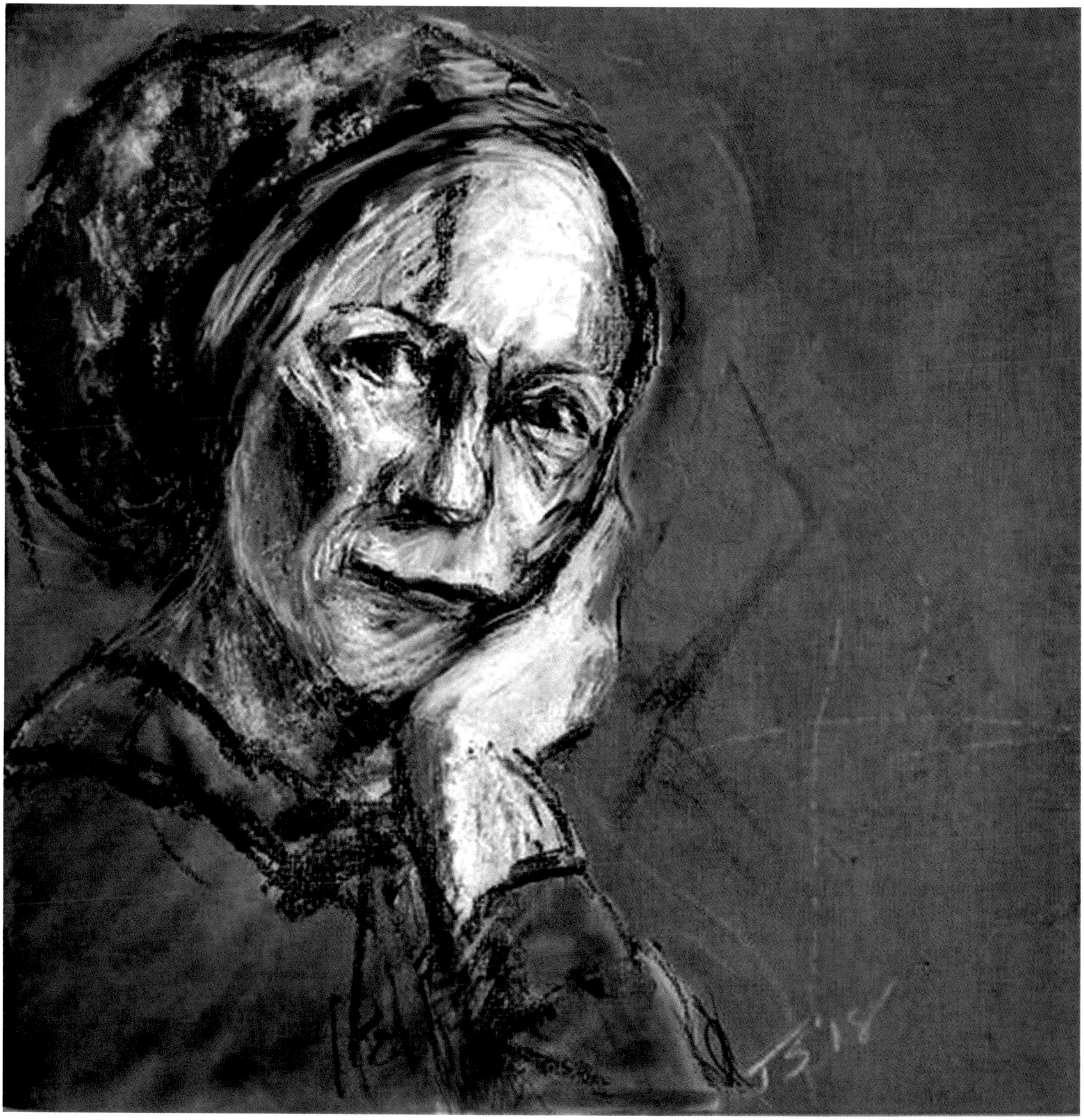

# COLORS

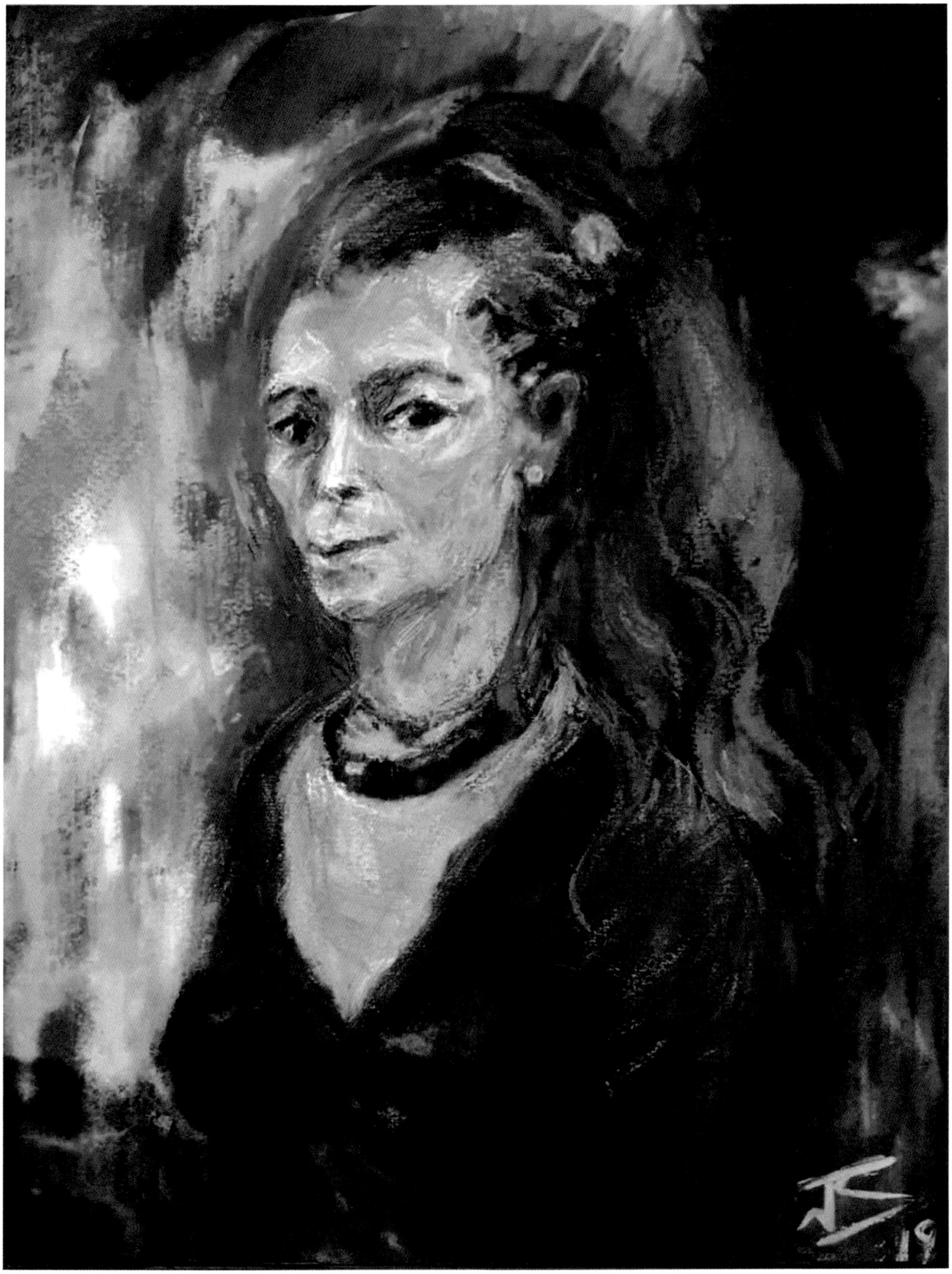

17. **Red** She has a deadset look, not to be fooled—that's her private self on the viewer's left side. The public self is a bit more vulnerable, and, at the corner of the mouth, there's a trace, possibly, from having smiled. The wit is there, French style, although it may not be surfaced at the moment. What most matters is the poetry of the colors—colors in her hair and complexion and in the dress that she chooses. The lit green in the background is like an attending angel, singing her red-orange hair.

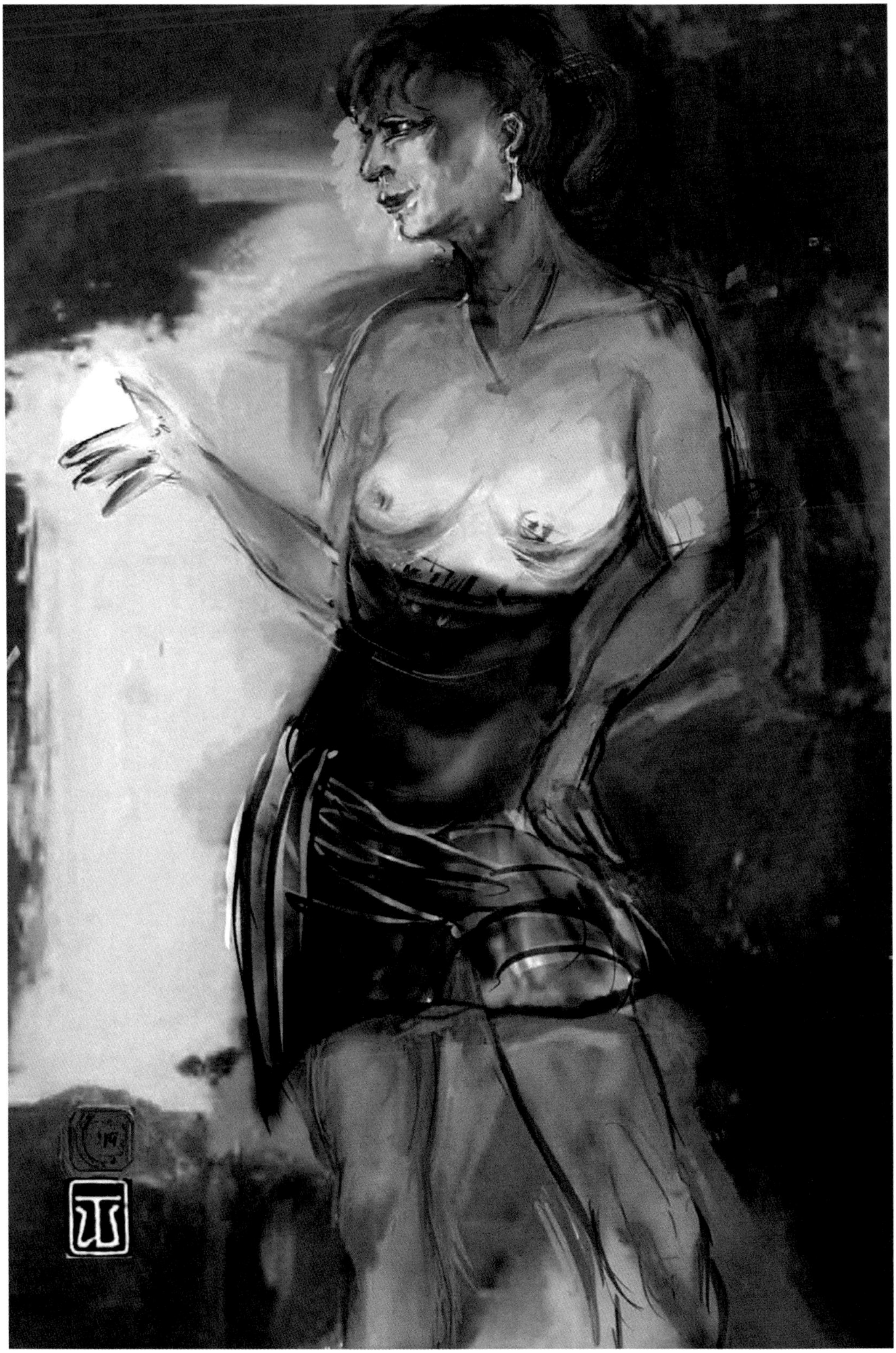

18. **Dancer in Leather** She has the strong legs of a dancer. Such a contrast with the usual vulnerable odalesque whose body asks only, without agency, for lovemaking. The painter's mark is visible in a hand completed just enough to carry the motion. What I enjoy about her and her world is the red-oranges and blue-greens, a nightclub's sexy low lights. I like the tough leather skirt, her neat confidant breasts, the way everything moves in the dance.

19. **Lorraine**

It's the wit and the irony, in the corner of the mouth, in the eyes. The hair is somewhat frazzled; it's a somewhat frazzled person, really. Perhaps she is a show-biz person (as this model really was.) You do not find her inhibited when she wants to enjoy the party. And you rarely find her fooled. Strong lighting does not discount her, because what she no longer has in youth, she still has in the sexiness of her personality. The small breasts too, they have held up. The painter is present, using a common enough trope—shadows on one side and lights on the other. Yet the watercolor variegation, that's different, and it somehow expresses the colors of our perceptive and gently mocking friend.

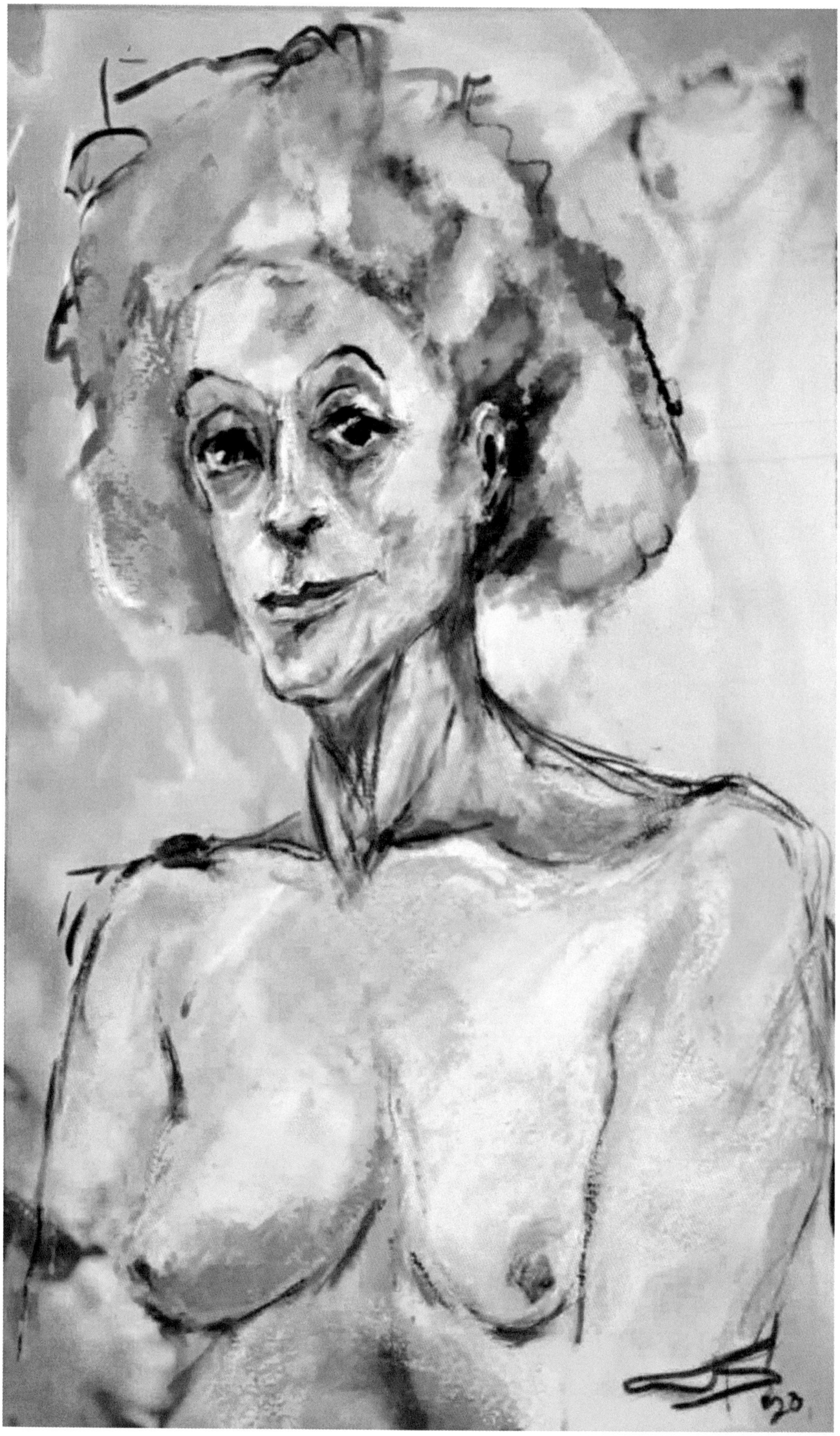

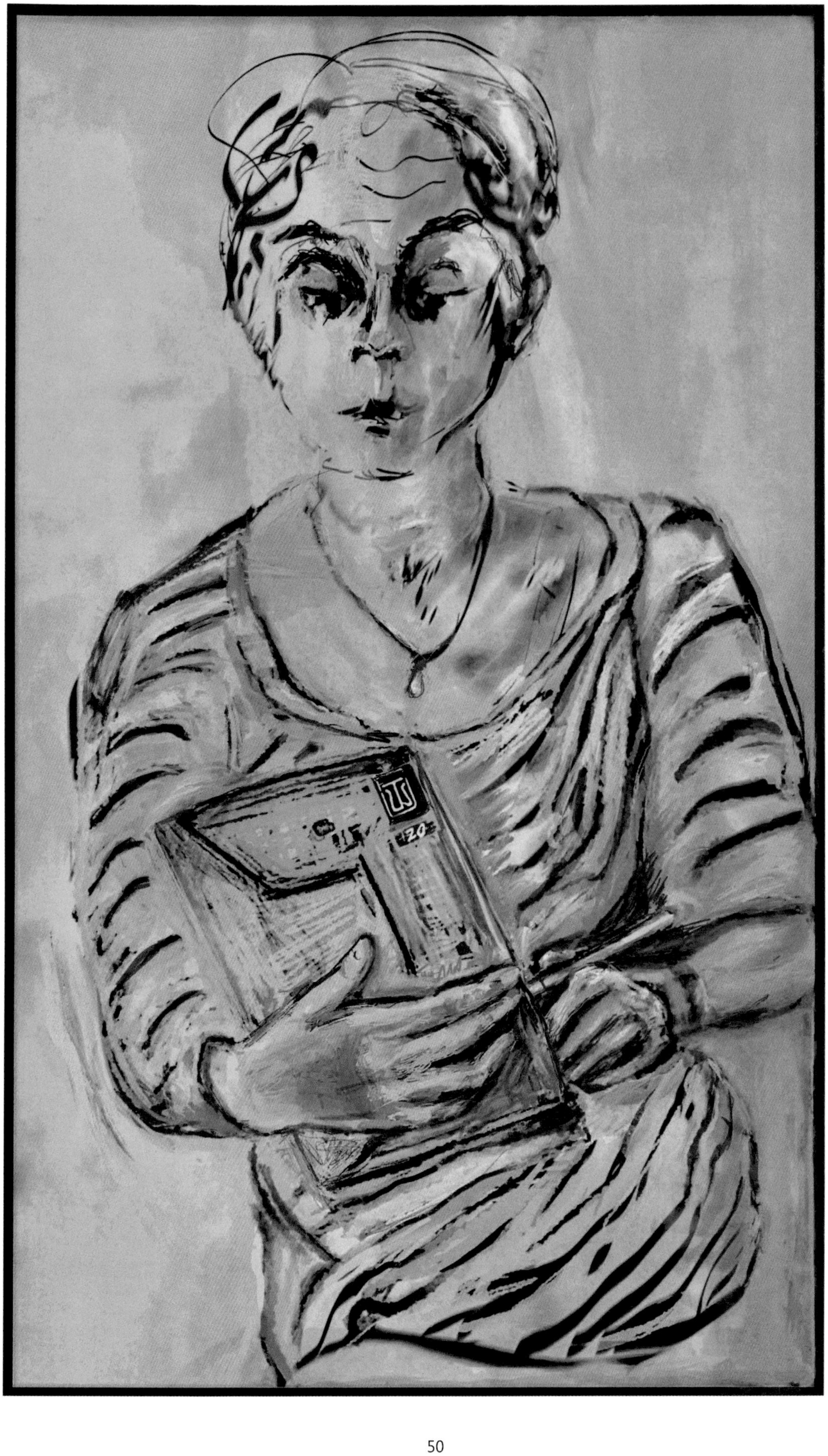

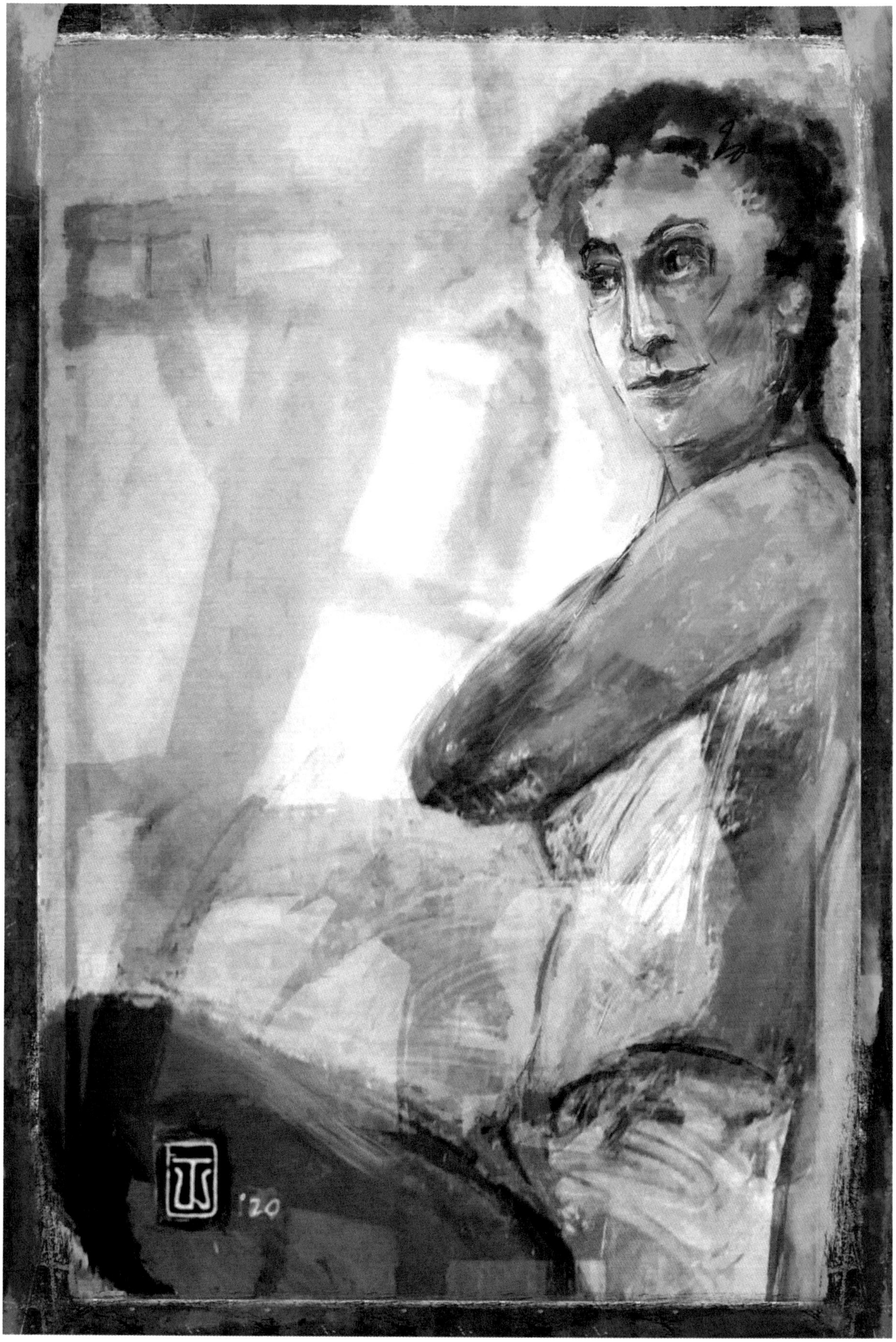

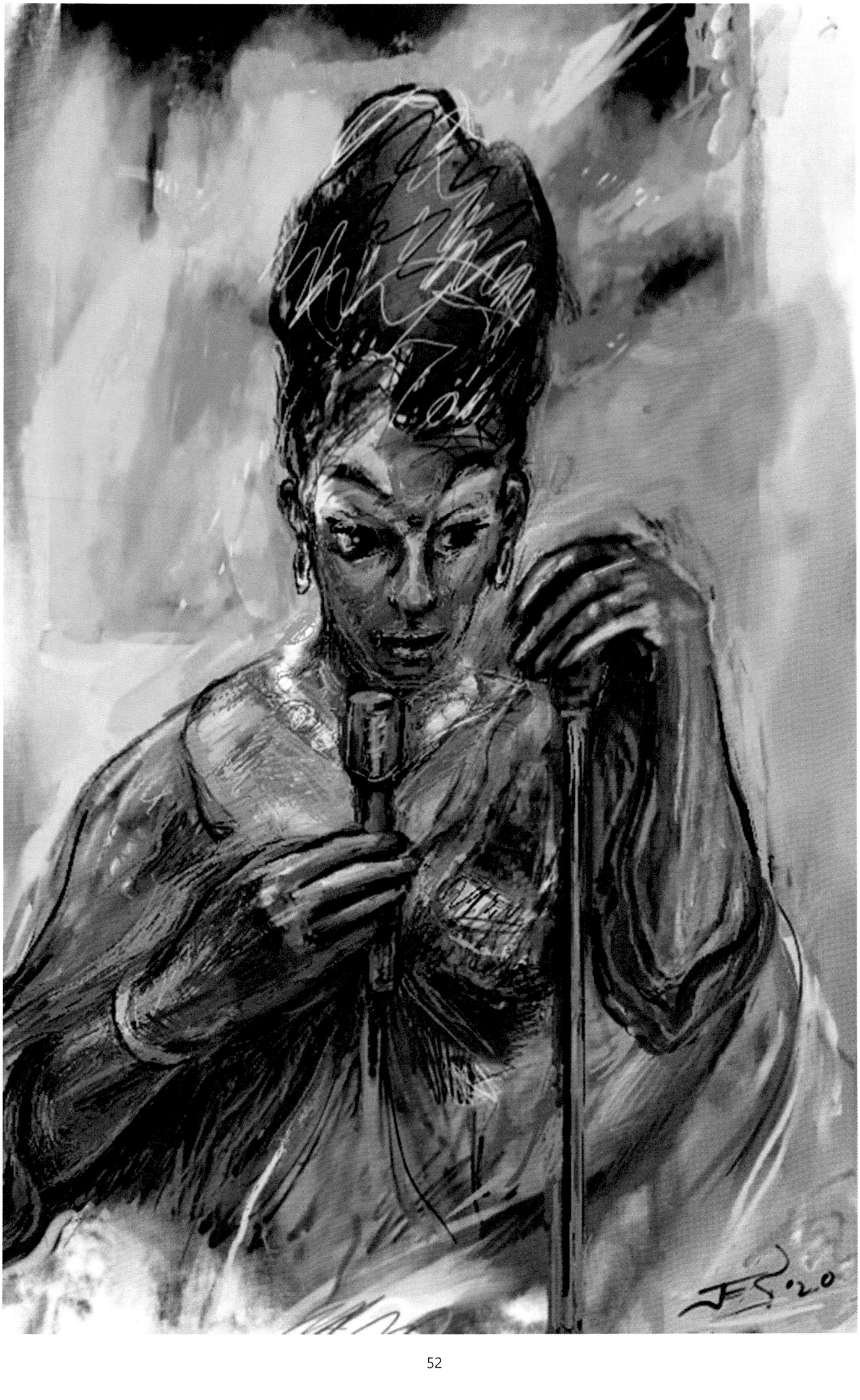

20.   PREVIOUS PAGES, LEFT: **iPad Artist, Red Case**

21.   PREVIOUS PAGES, RIGHT: **Jemmie**

22.   **A Lady Sings the Blues**

23.   **The Long Road Home**

## 24.  Mercutio

In *Romeo and Juliet,* Mercutio is the cherished and cherishing cousin of Romeo. He is a joker, killed in clan fighting at a tragically young age.

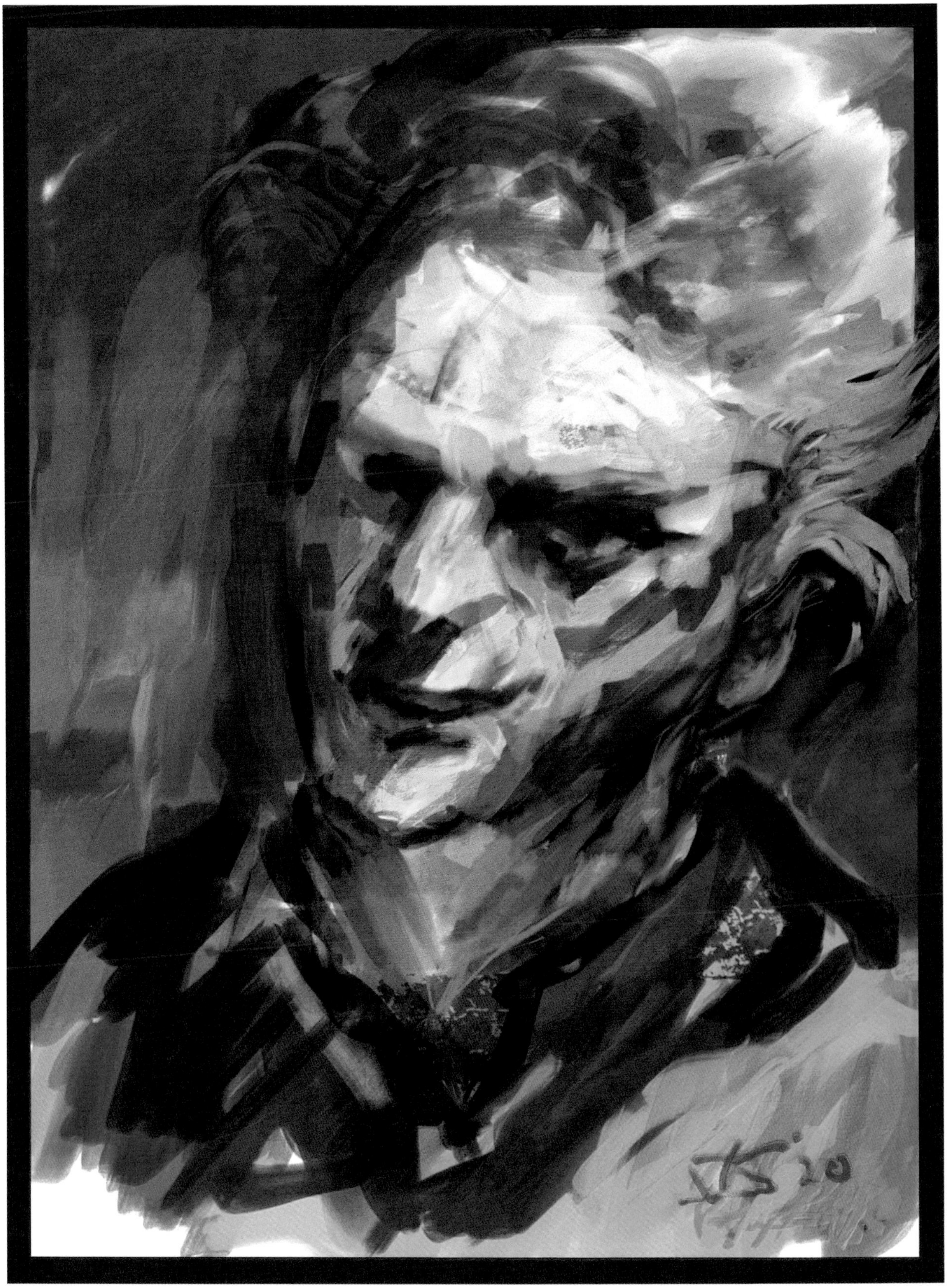

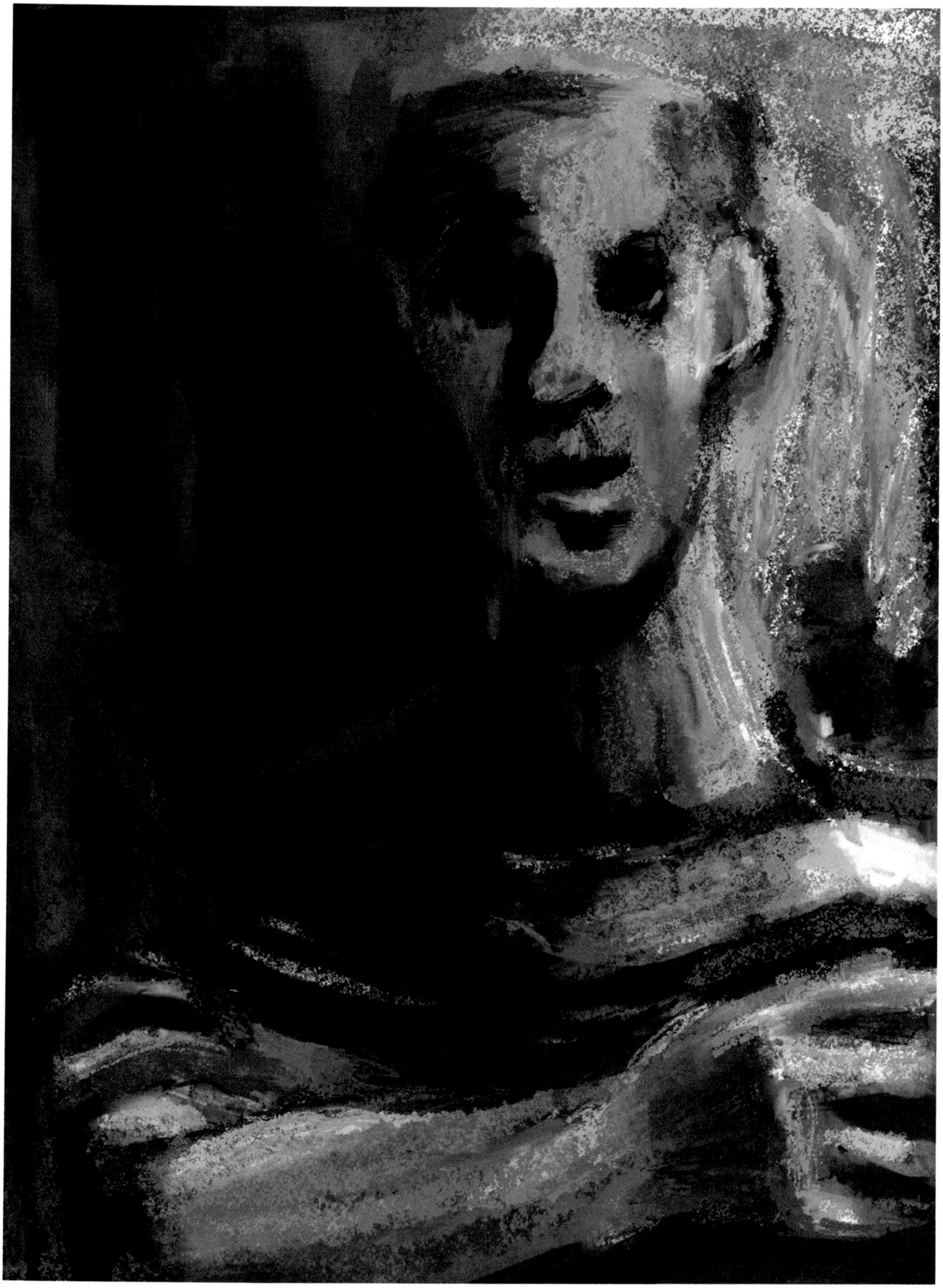

25. **Alex, Arms Crossed (Homage Park).** Alex and Jen are more solid and sculptural than most in this collection, with its accent on the diaphanous. That is because they are inspired by the work of David Park, who, early in his career, carved stone for the WPA. Alex differs from his

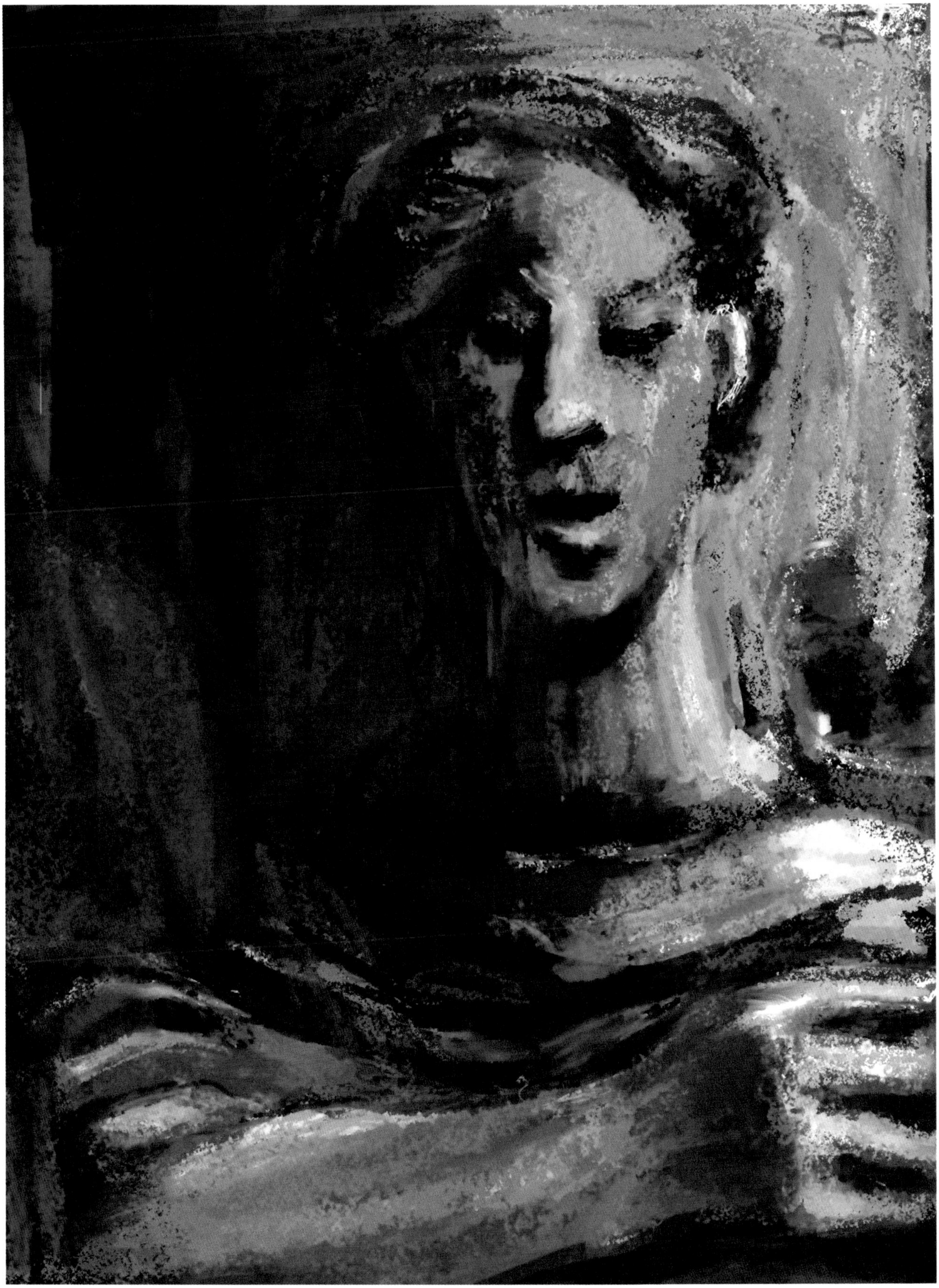

Park antecedent because Park's **Boy in Striped Shirt** inhabits a mask-like face. **Alex** is, on the contrary, as alive and "right *there*" as I could make him. **Jen, Sculptor (Homage Park)** (26.) is gender-fluid; she has the strong hands of a stone carver.

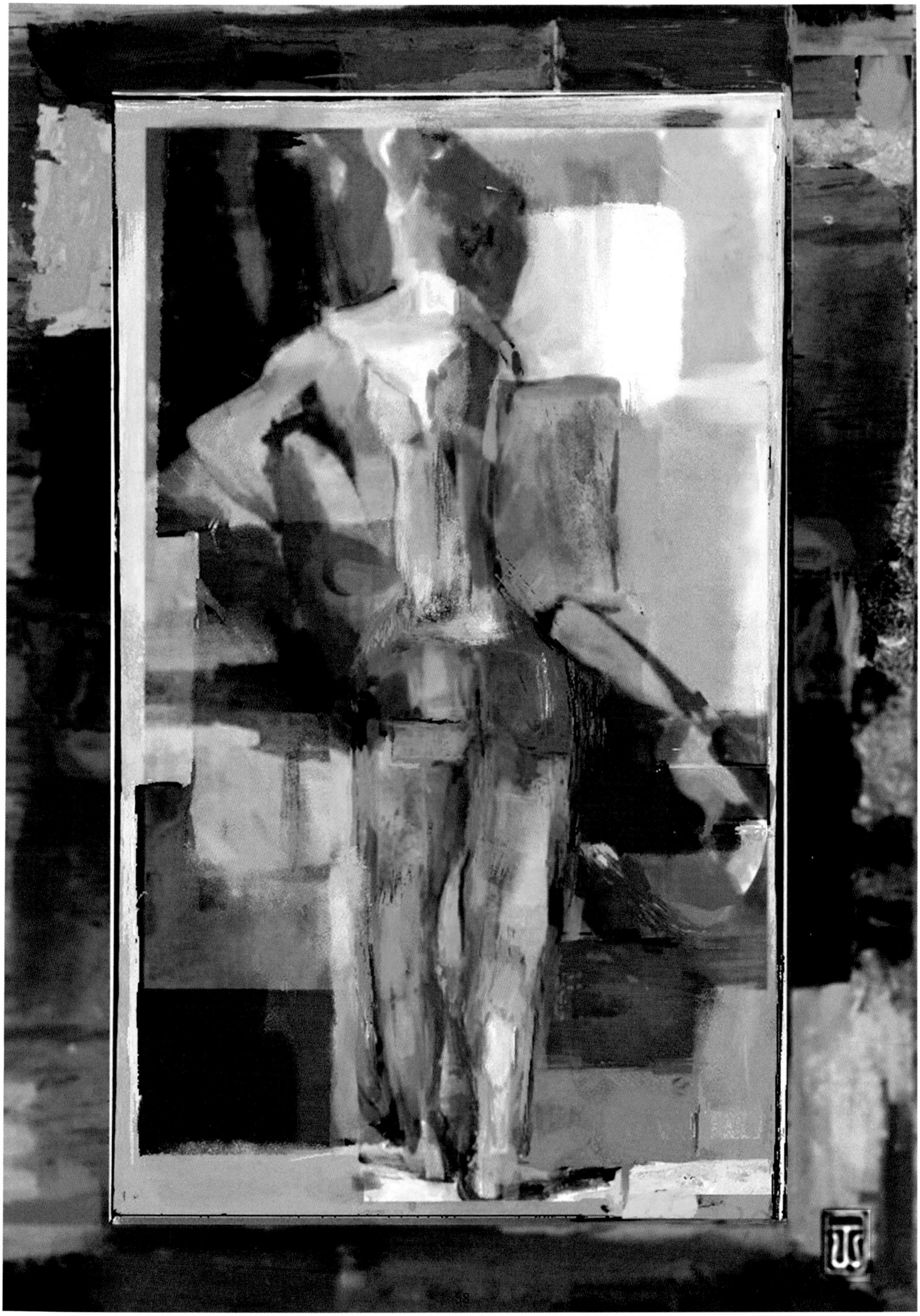

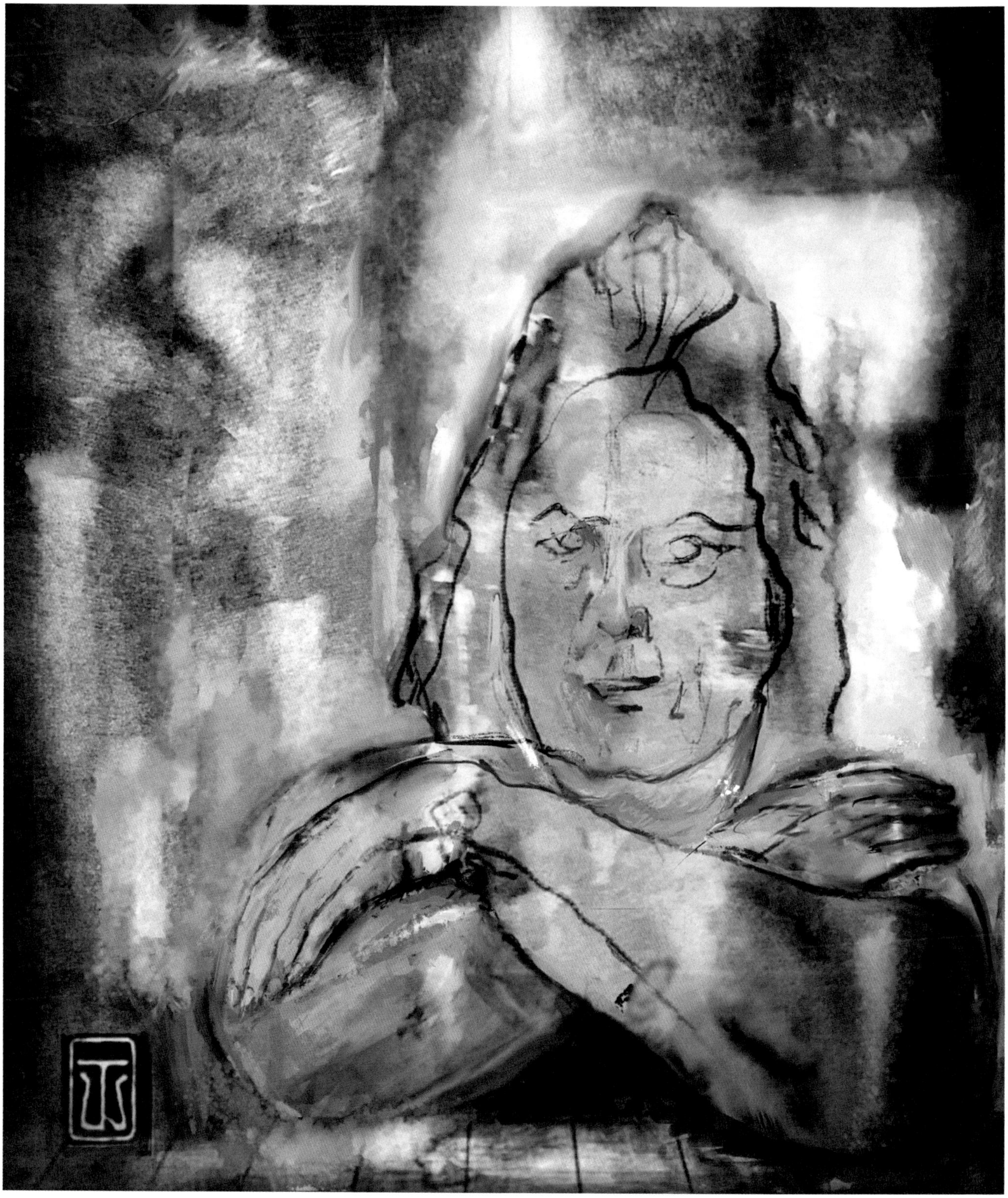

27 **Framed Figure**

28. **A Life in Theatre**

What follows is a series of abstracts I completed during the same COVID timespan that gave rise to many of the Late Style portraits. These abstracts share features with the portraits: intersecting worlds; a suggestion that one might be vulnerable to something mysterious, waiting in the wings. And yet these qualities coexist, in the abstracts, with a certain vivacious intensity, the unabashed assertions of color . . .

# ABSTRACTS

## 29.  **There Is Often a Way Out**

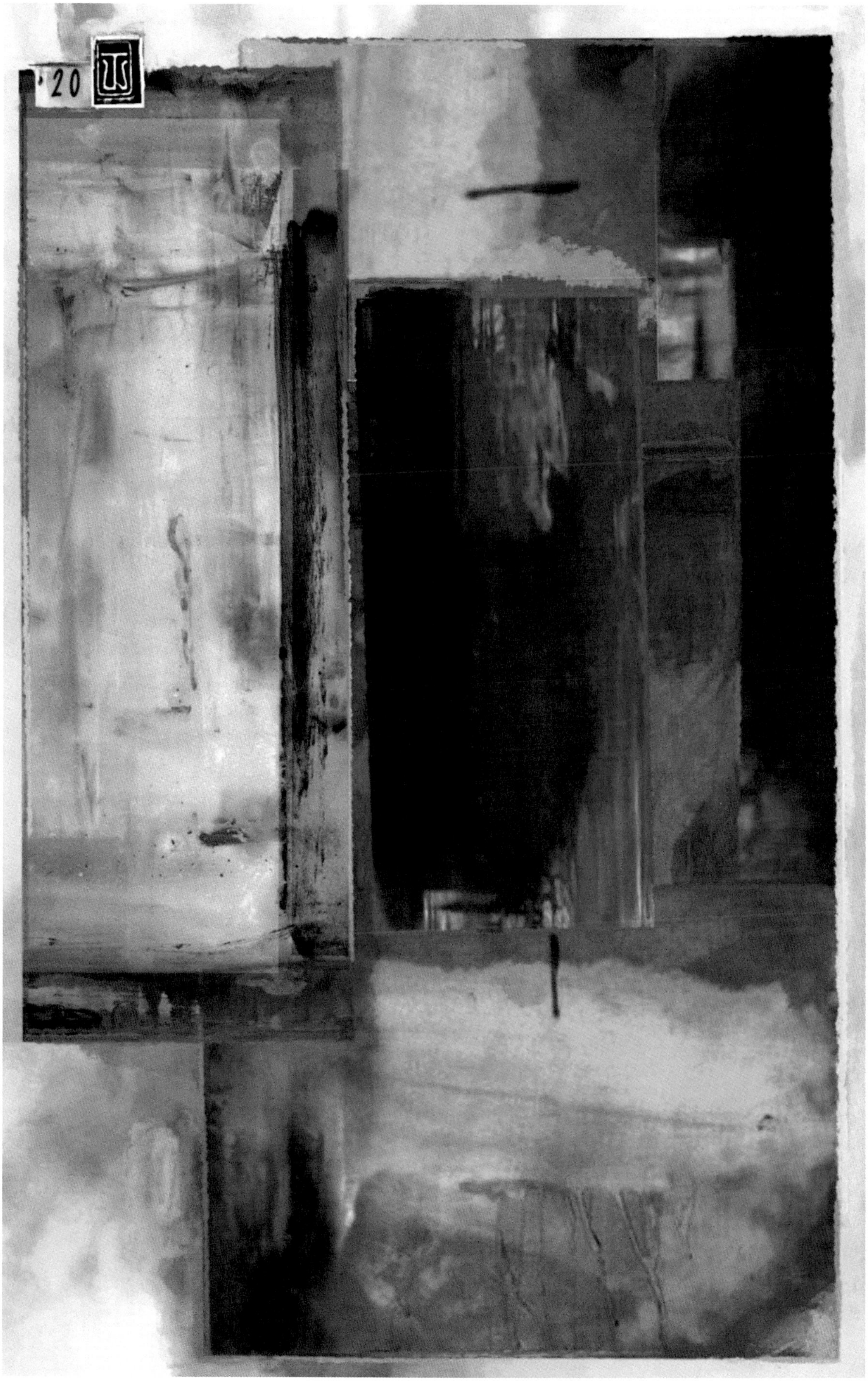
'20

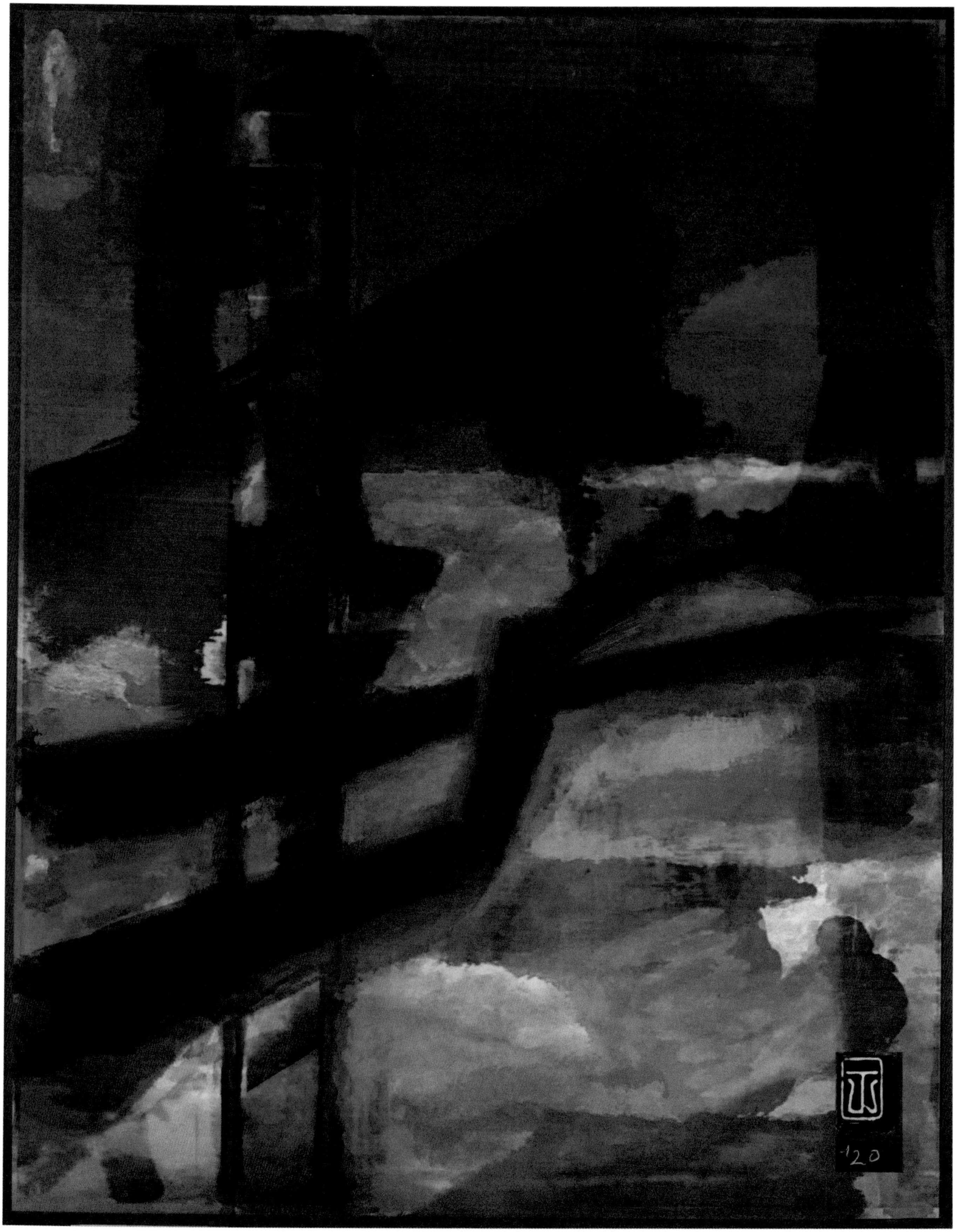

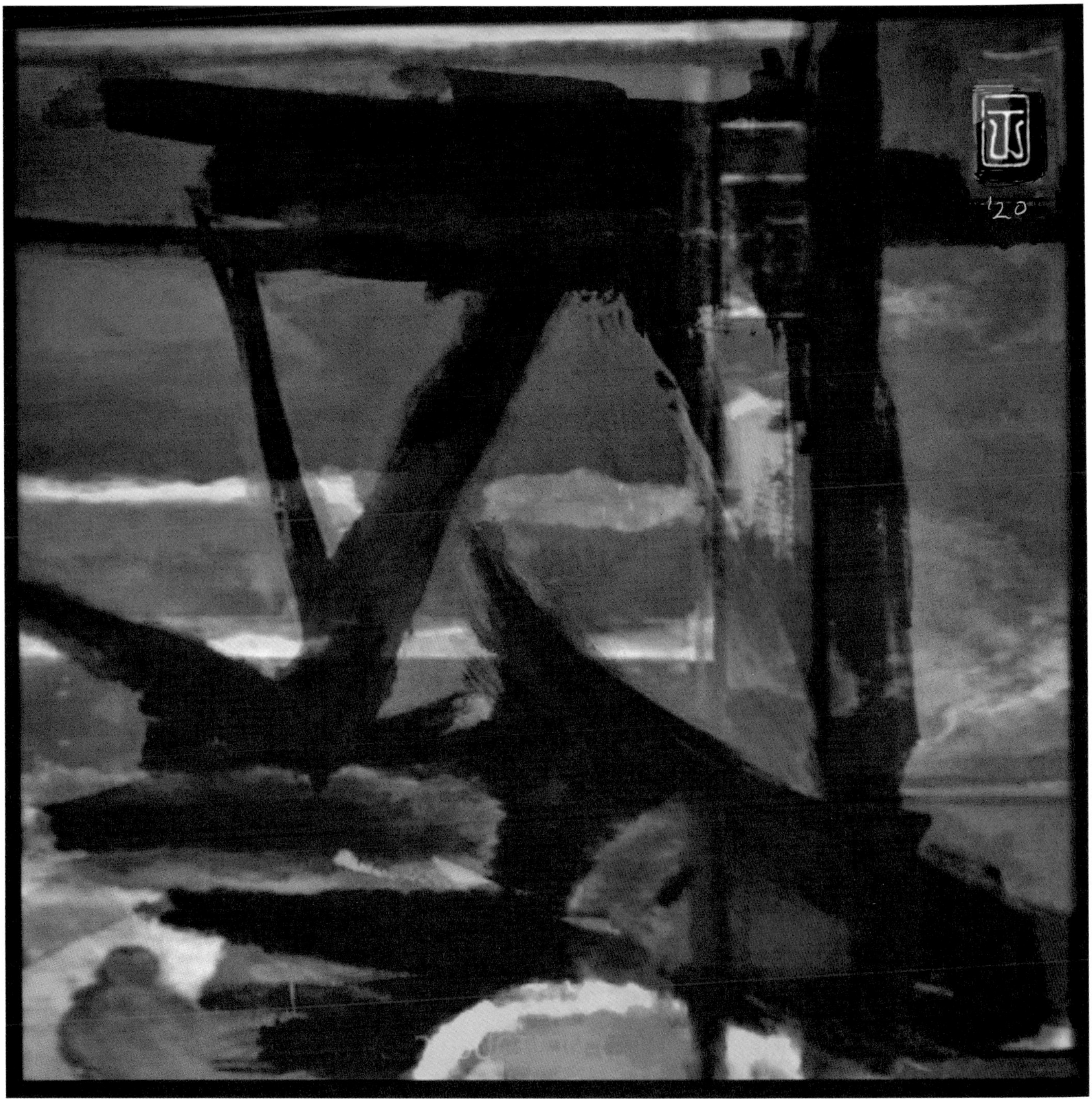

30. **Bridge into Night** (ACROSS)

31. **Boardwalk Memories** (ABOVE)

32. **Figure at the Window** (ABOVE)

33. **Door Underwater** (ACROSS)

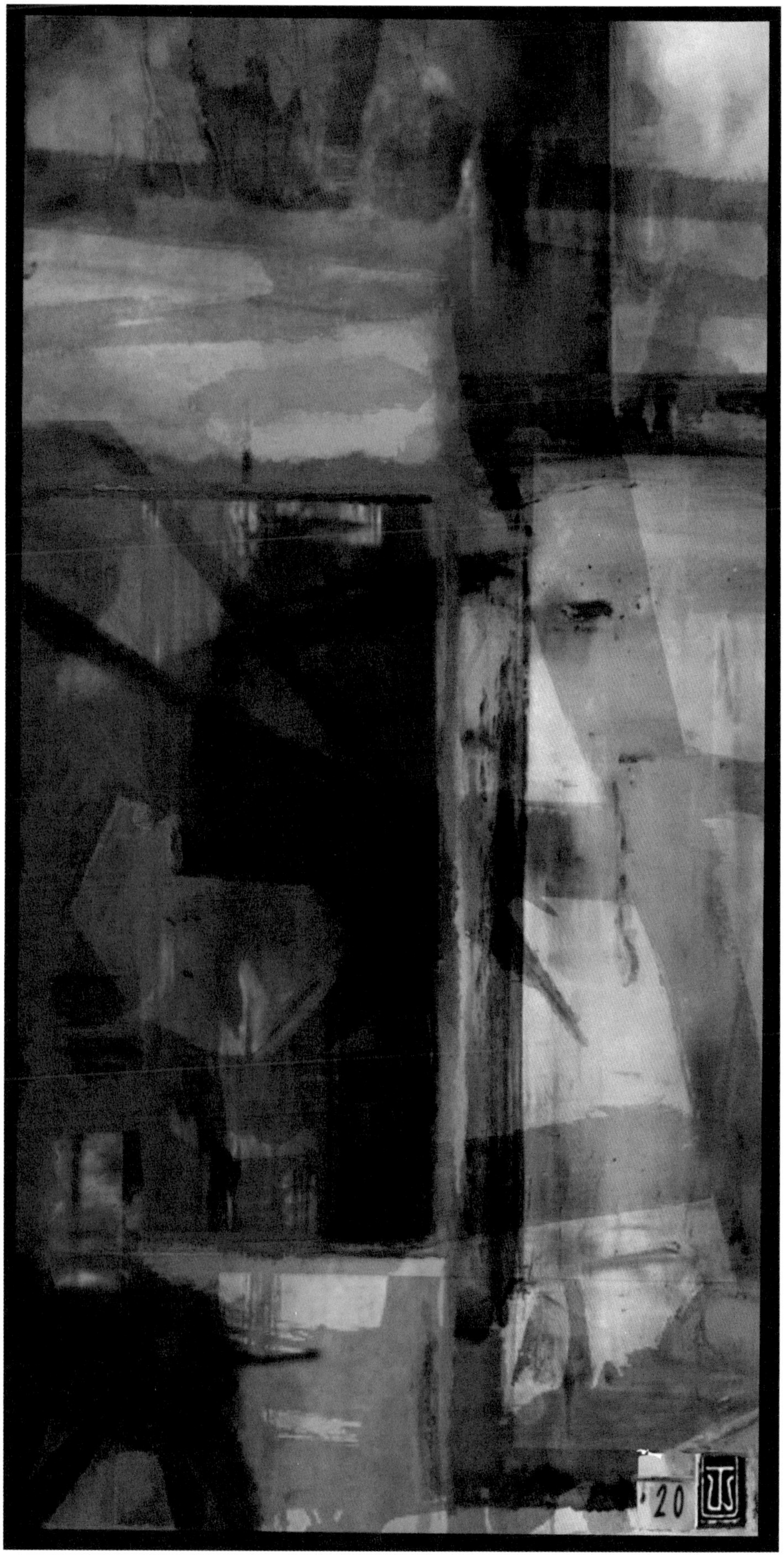
'20

34. **Steppin' Out**

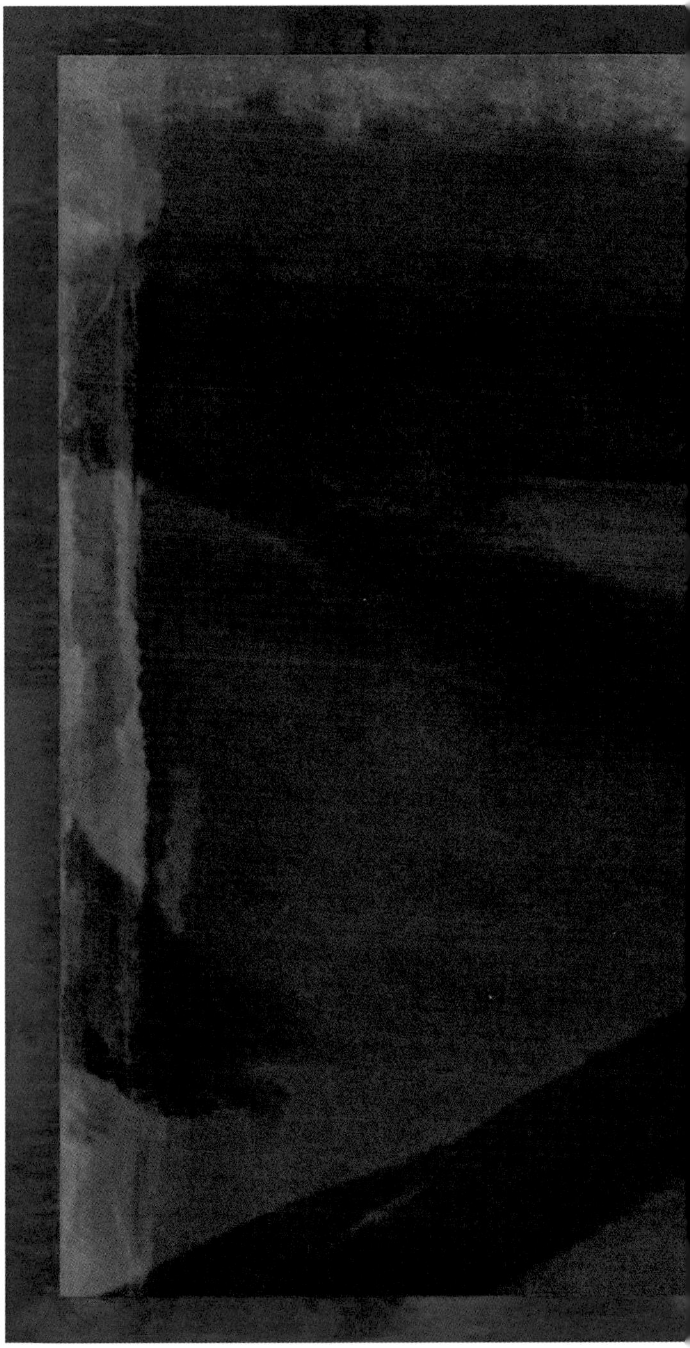

35. **Parting**

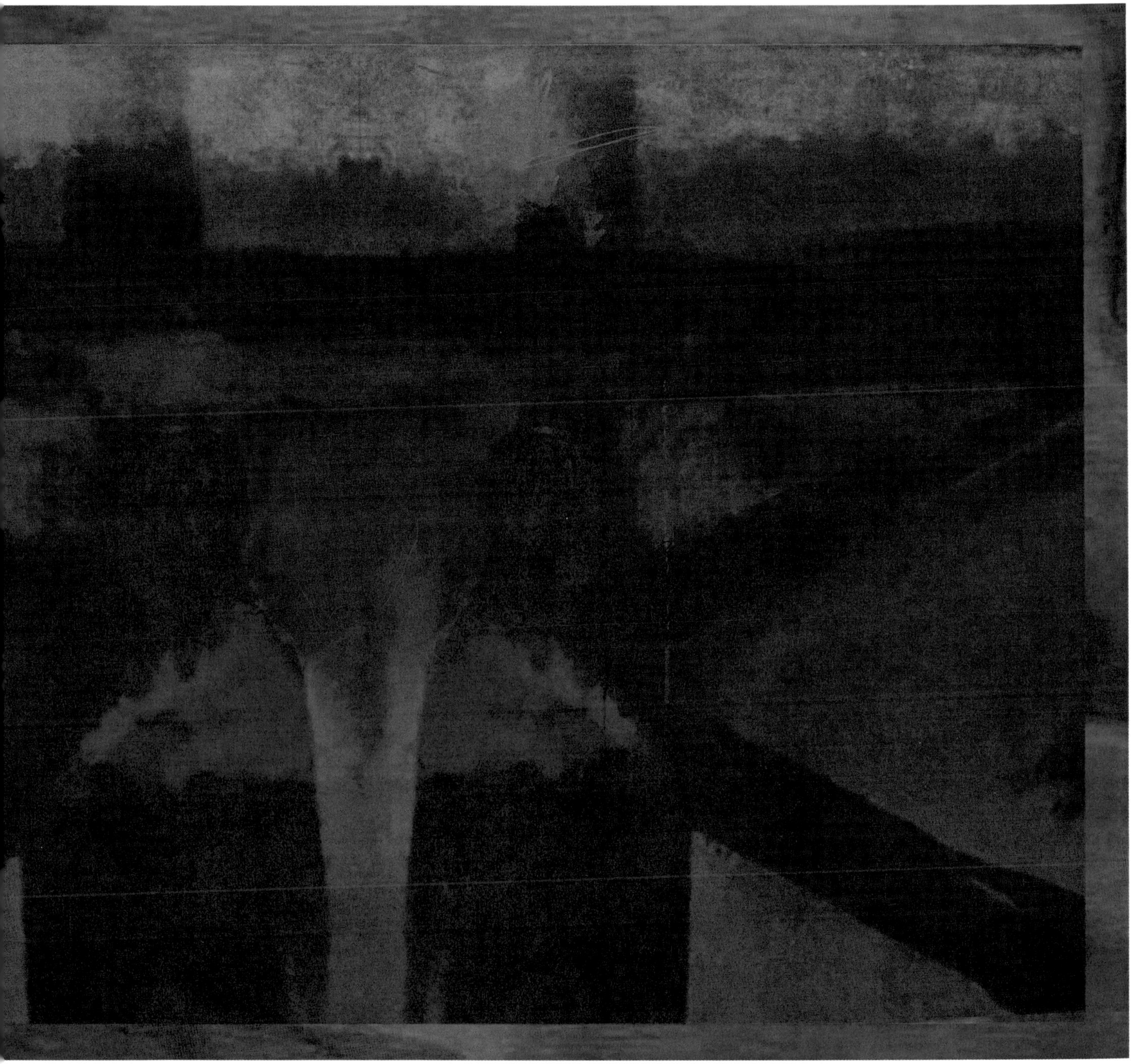

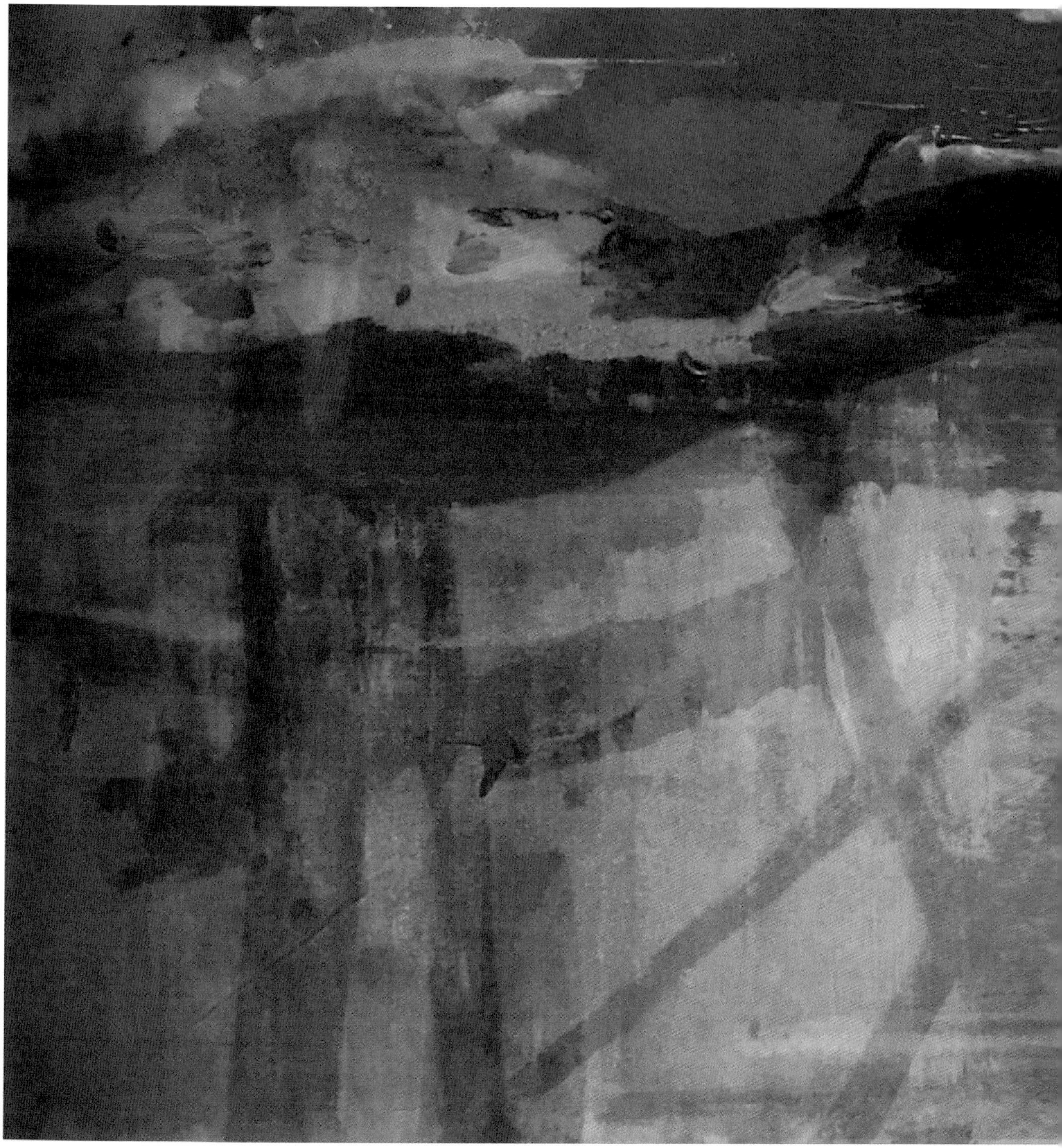

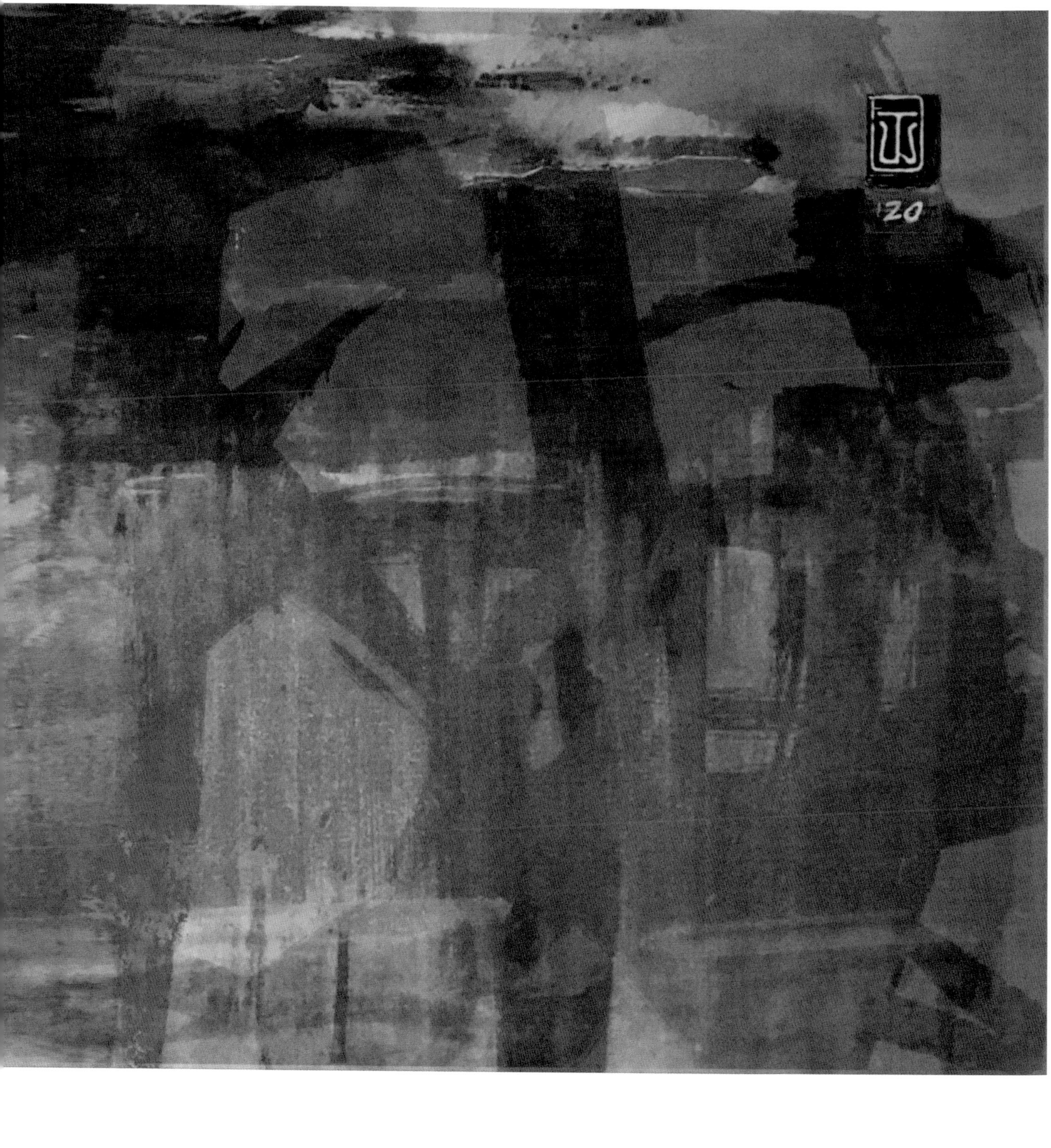

36. **Ancient Lake**

# MARKS—CHARCOAL, PASTEL, INK

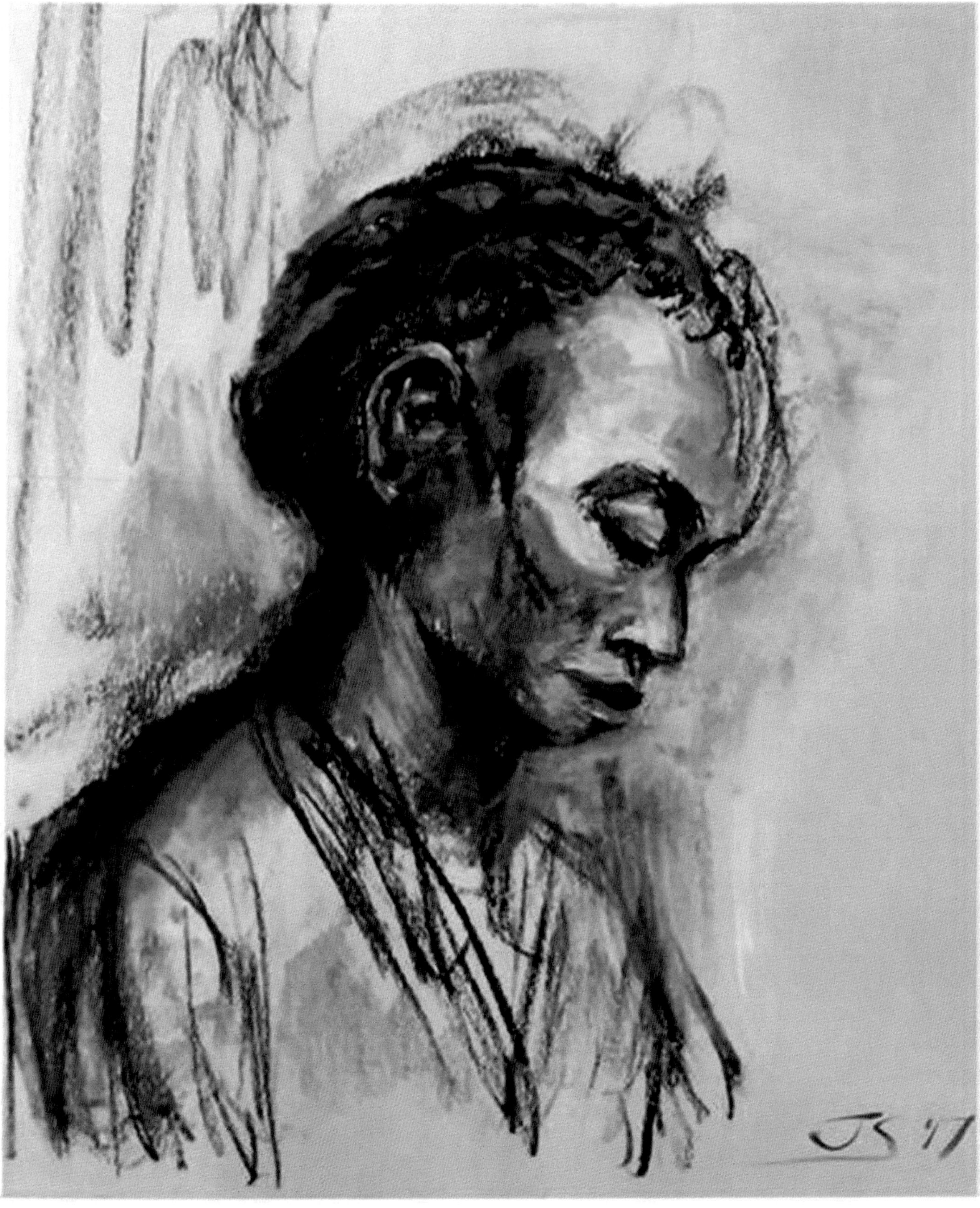

37. **My Unconquerable Soul**

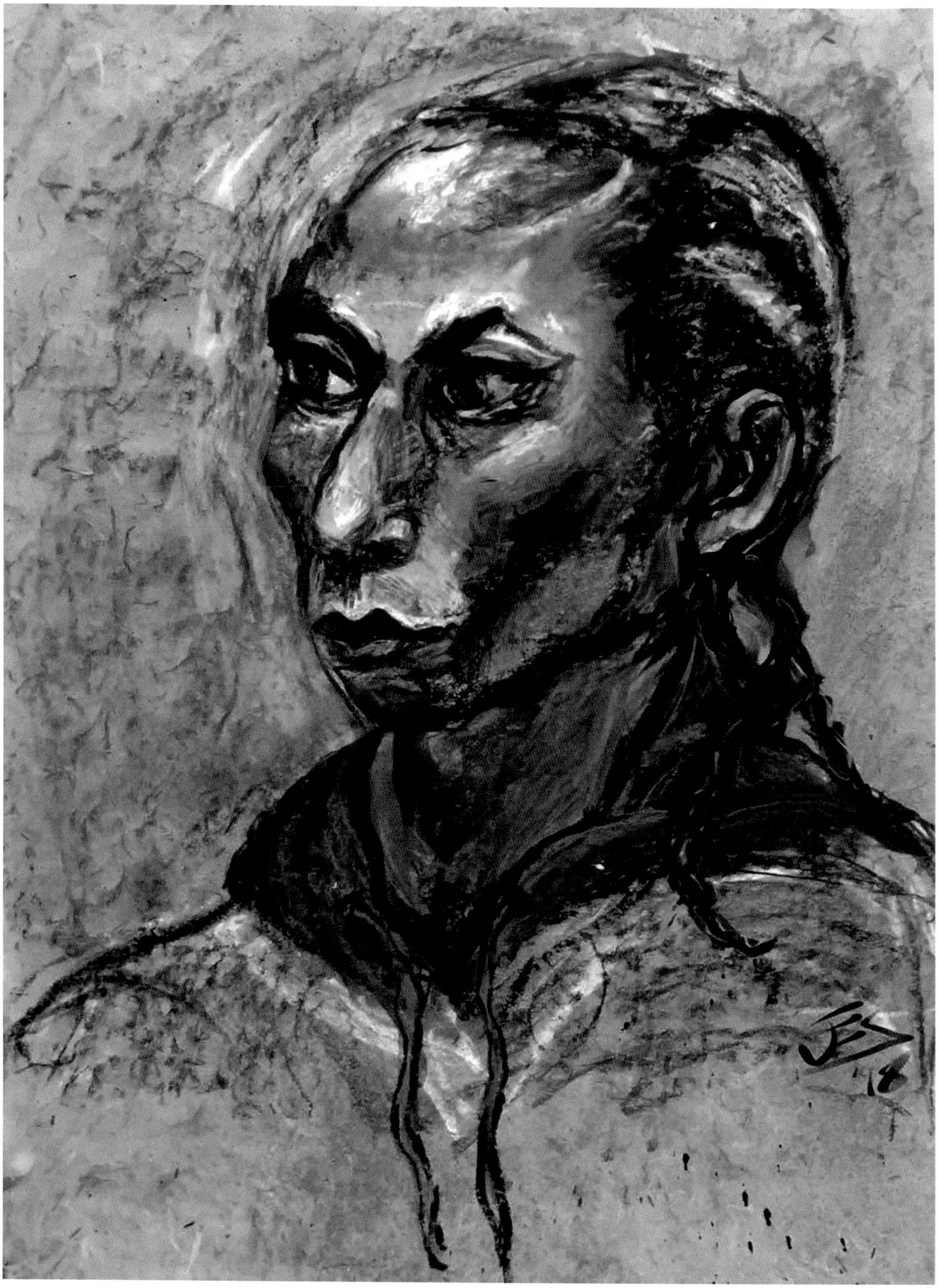

38. **Brian in a Red Hoodie**

"My unconquerable soul" (37.) is taken from *Invictus* by William Ernest Henley. The first verse begins with "Out of the night that covers me..." The poem ends with "I thank whatever gods may be/ For my unconquerable soul."

Four images that happen to portray black Americans have been grouped here in the section called **Marks**. Why? They have a drawn quality about them, a prominent artist's mark.

To my mind there is a dear beauty in these models. I especially love the young woman depicted on this page. I have seen her through different incarnations, but this particular one I'll call (39.) **Teresa with Big Hair**.

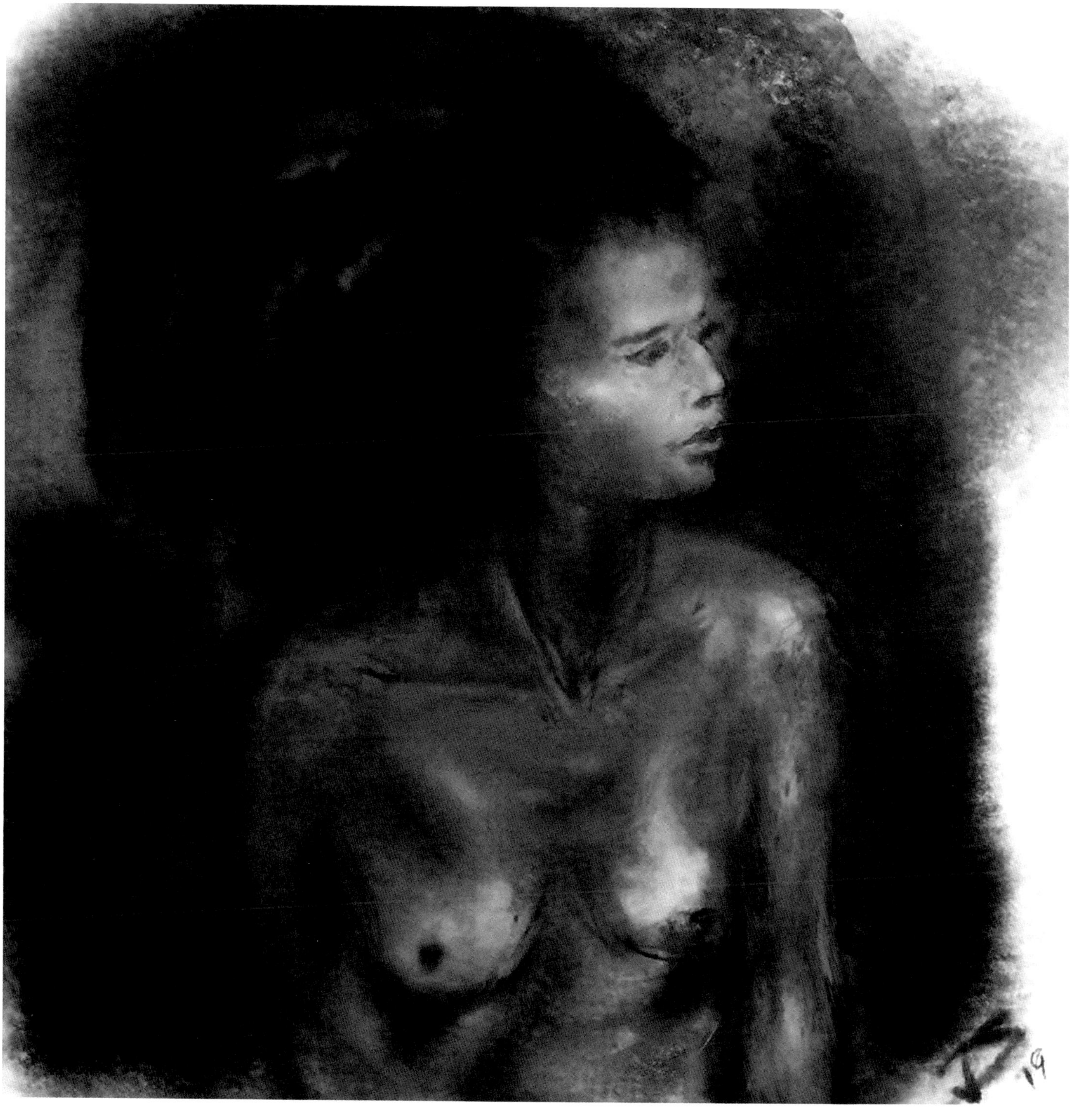

## 40.  Man Looking Up

I appreciate the enduring character as it shows itself in Jerry's facial bones. Apparently, when he was young, he excelled in track. He told me this when one of my versions of him caught a youthful zest that lingered in the older man. He said he used to look that way at the start of a race. Now he is a grandfather.

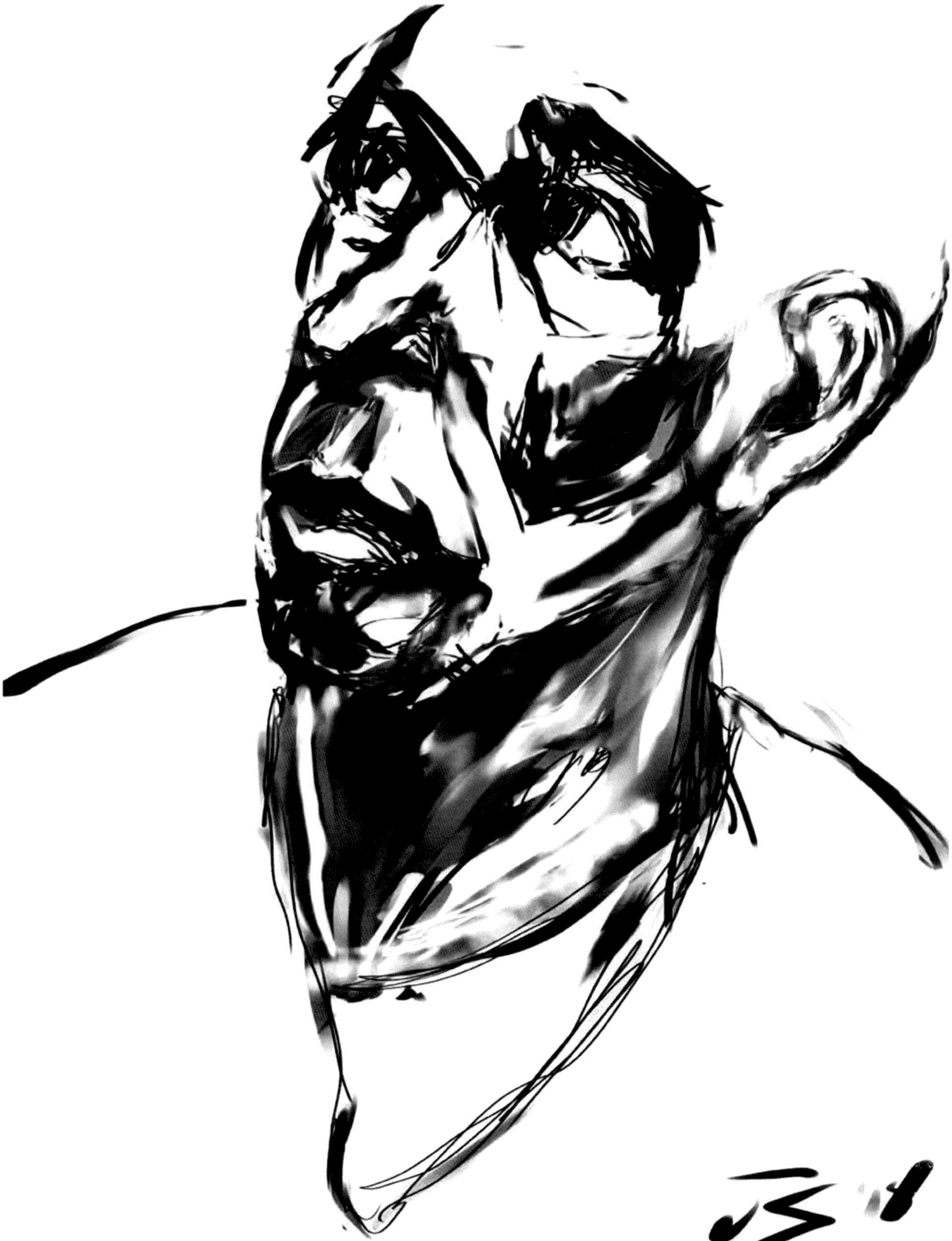

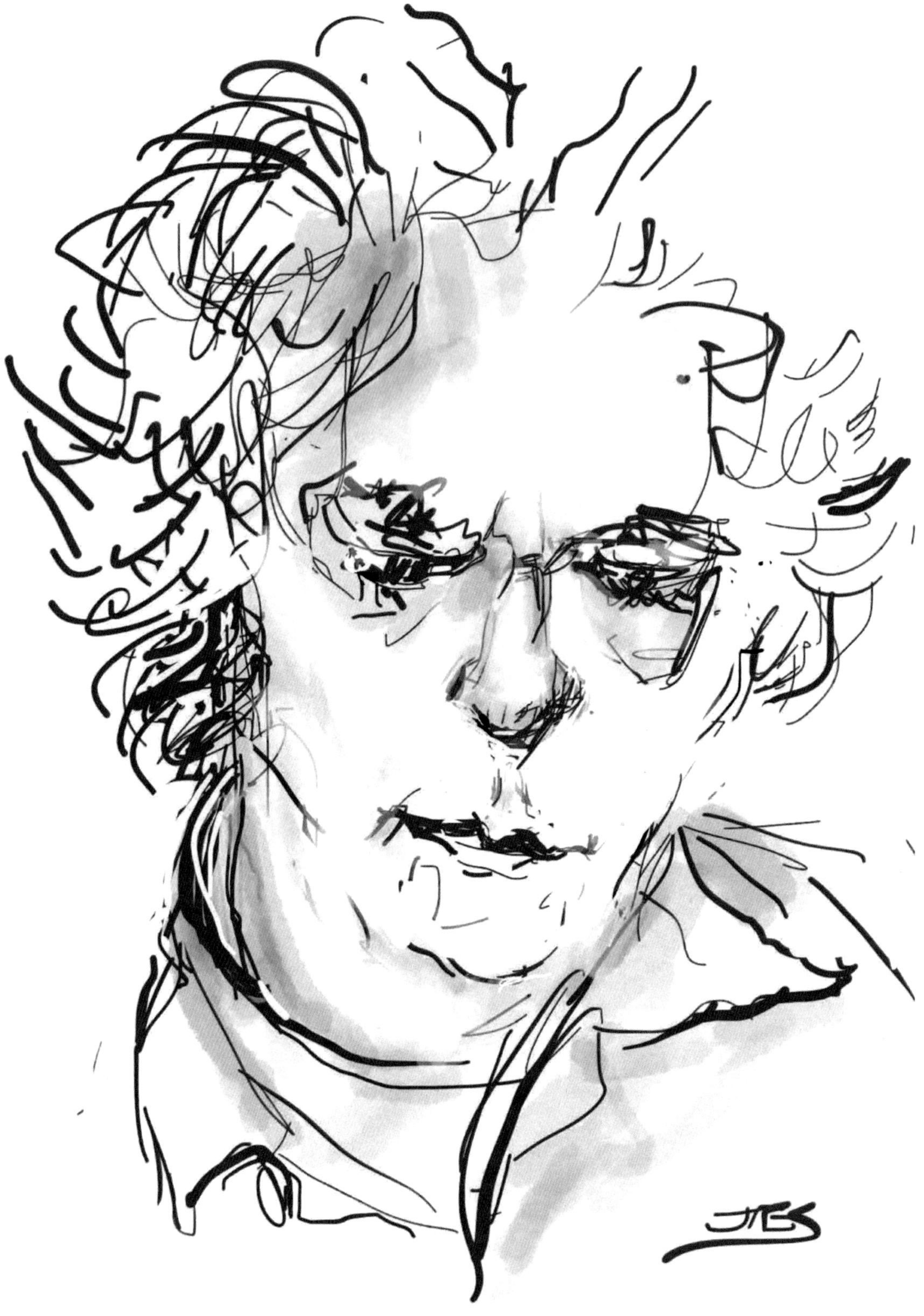

41. **Judith as Beethoven** (ABOVE). Broody, with more than a hint of the tragic. The hair so much a part of the music of her. 42. **Judith in Sepia (**ACROSS)—the formidable intelligence**.**

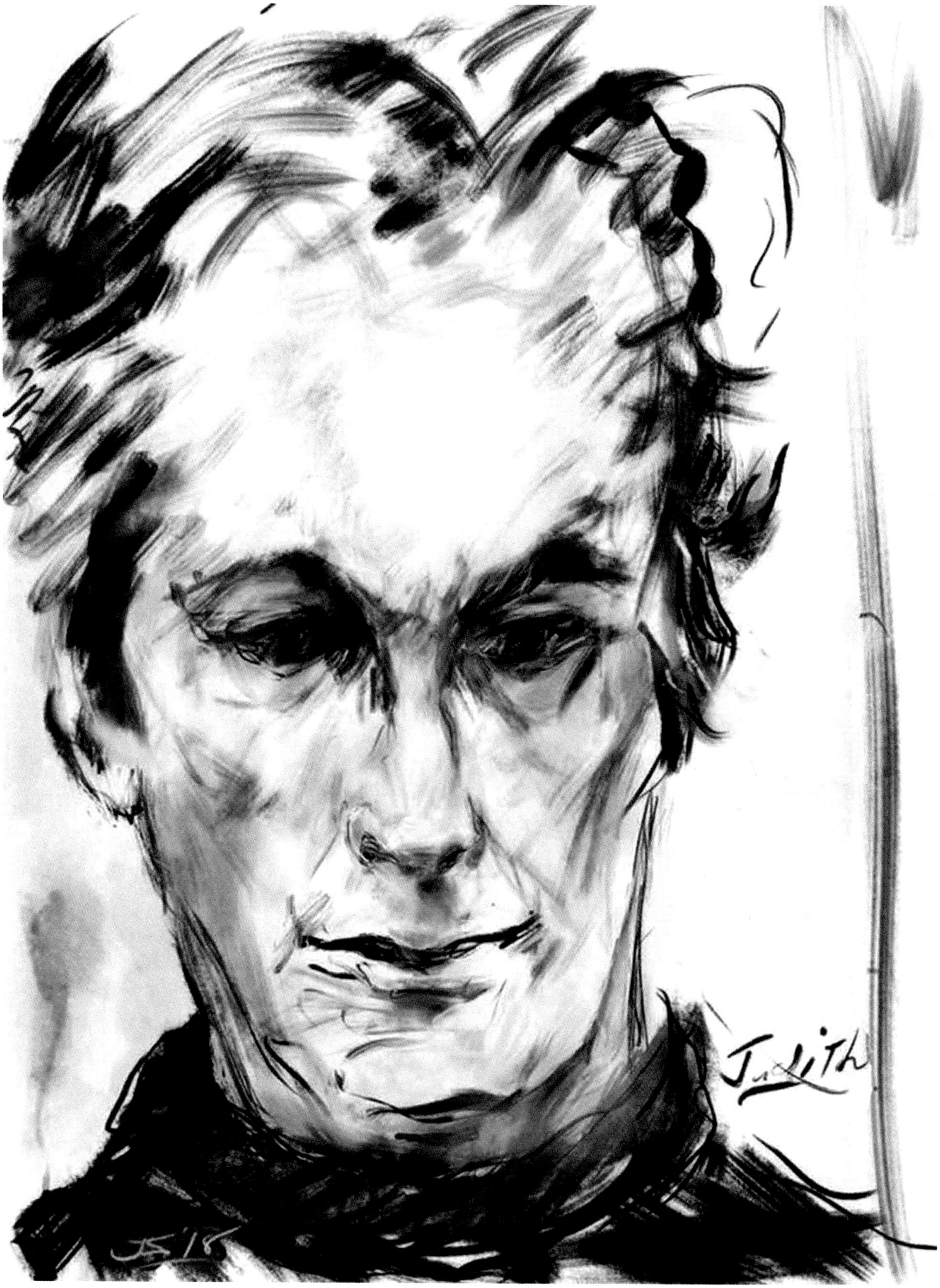
Judith
JS '18

### 43.   Myself as a Man

I began drawing on my iPad at noon. As the day wore on, the light receded; the shadows shifted; my stylus scurried to keep up. I discovered that I had somehow, along the way, acquired the nose of my father. I assign blame or credit for this event, not just to family memory, but to the Fayum mummy portraits (from a Romanized Egypt). They lurked in my subconscious. I loved the noses—often invoked with a dark slash. There is Semitic blood in the Jews; in the Egyptians as well. So my stylus, like a wand, may have summoned the old tribes. In any case, it seemed, as the day wore on and the lights kept changing, I had become a man.

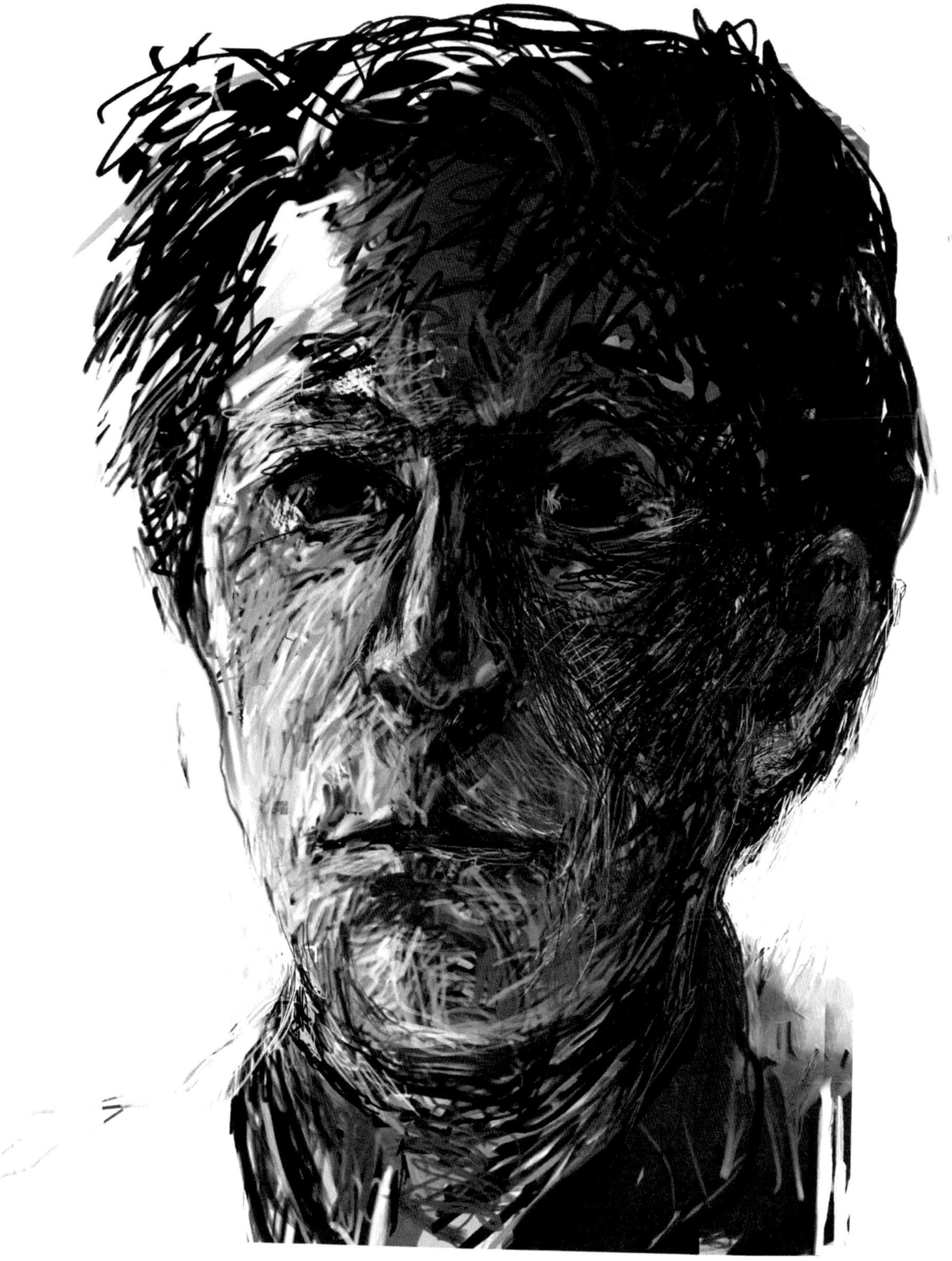

**44.  Edith in Black & White**

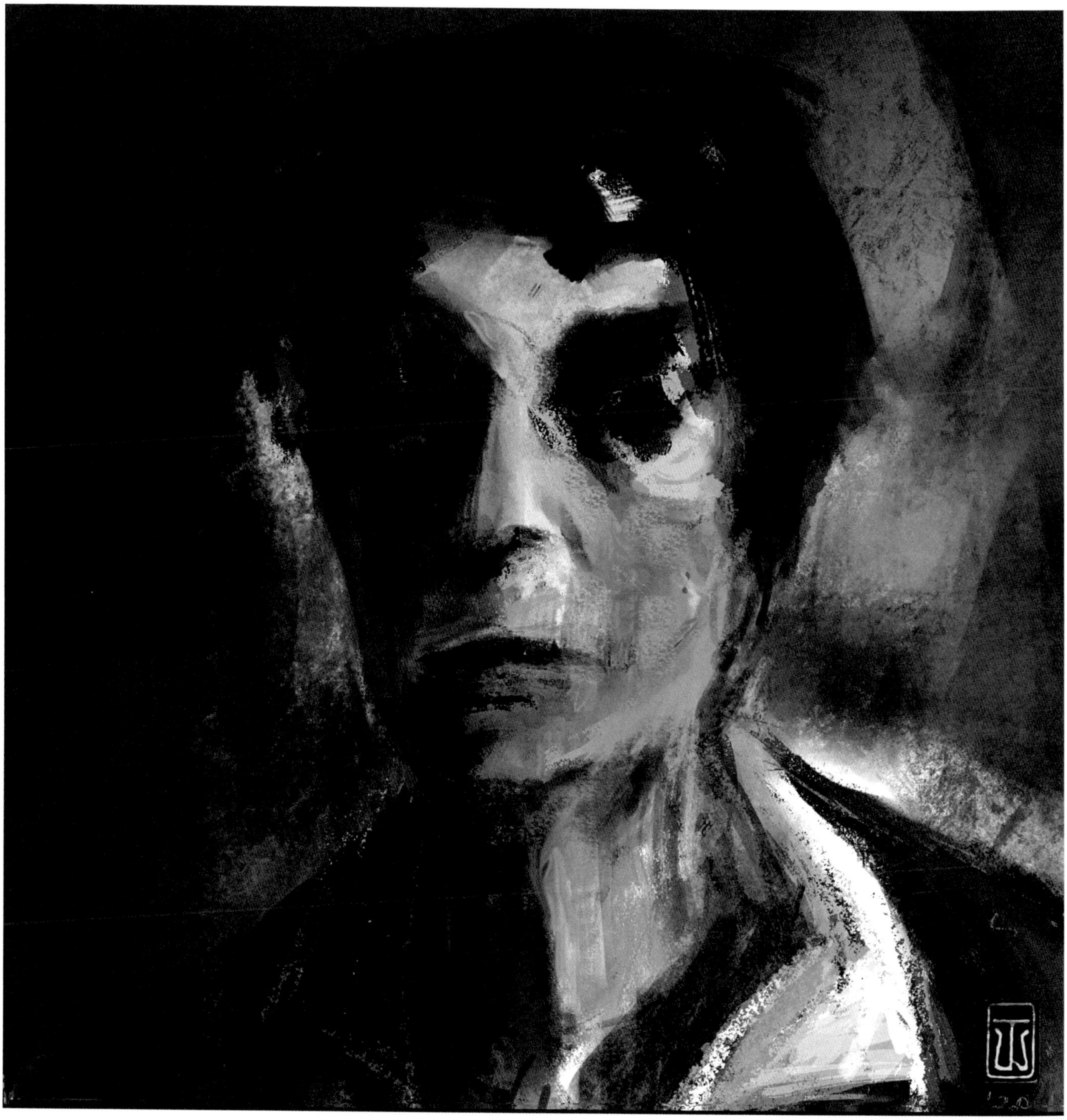

# TALES AND FAMILIARS

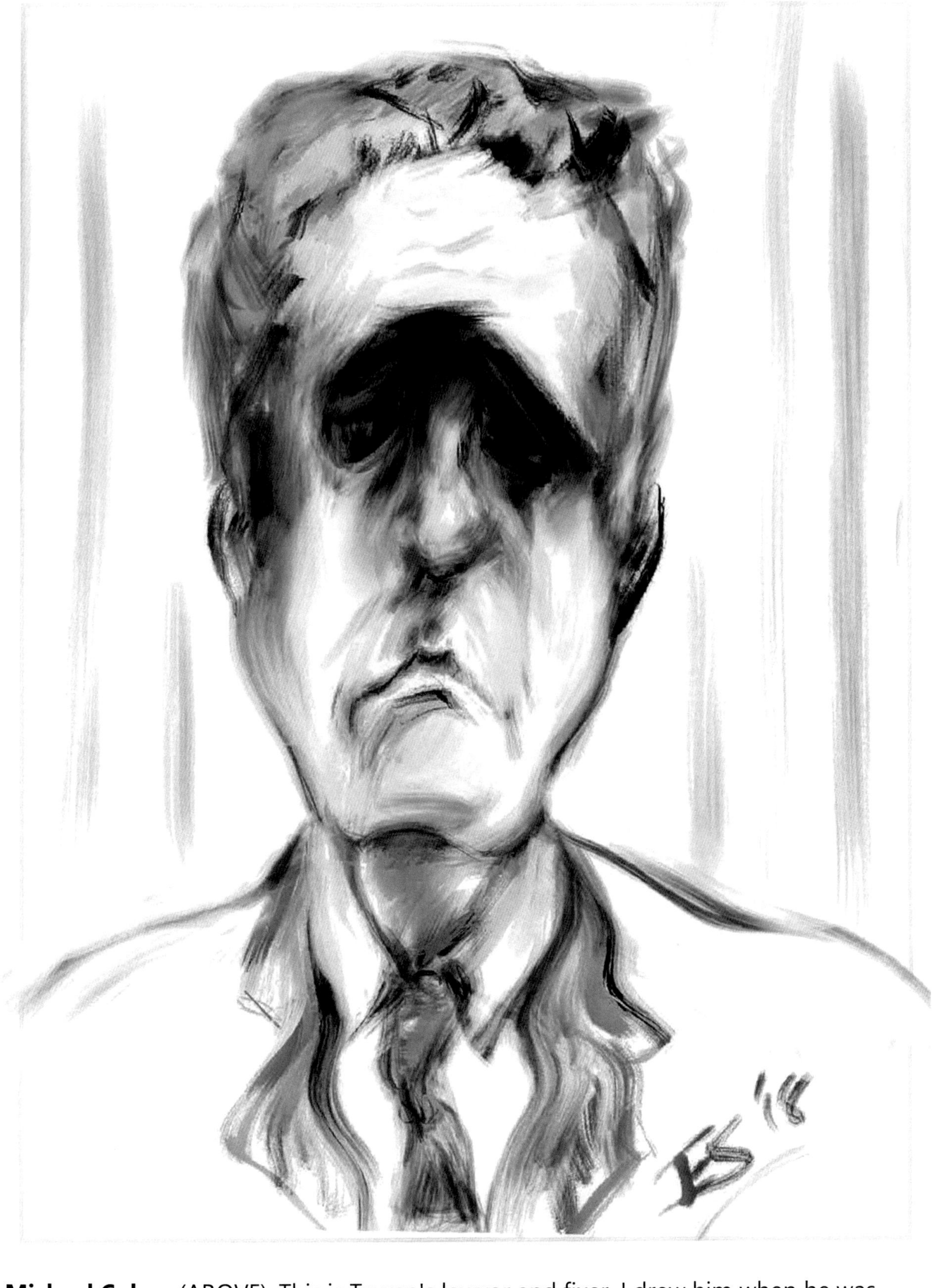

45. **Michael Cohen** (ABOVE). This is Trump's lawyer and fixer. I drew him when he was testifying to Congress. His face, I was thinking, is the saddest face I ever saw. (46.) **Rachel Maddow** (ACROSS)**.** Wildly intelligent, doggedly curious, she'd wear herself to a nub to get the answers. She is usually quite a wiseacre. But here I aimed to capture as

well her anxiety as she reports certain stories. During early COVID-19 she could have been mistaken for that distressed and angry prophet, Jeremiah, except that Jeremiah specialized in opinion and Rachel assailed her tribes with fact. She has confessed, no surprise, that she suffers bouts of depression. I love—and chose to draw out, literally— an androgynous aspect of her beauty.

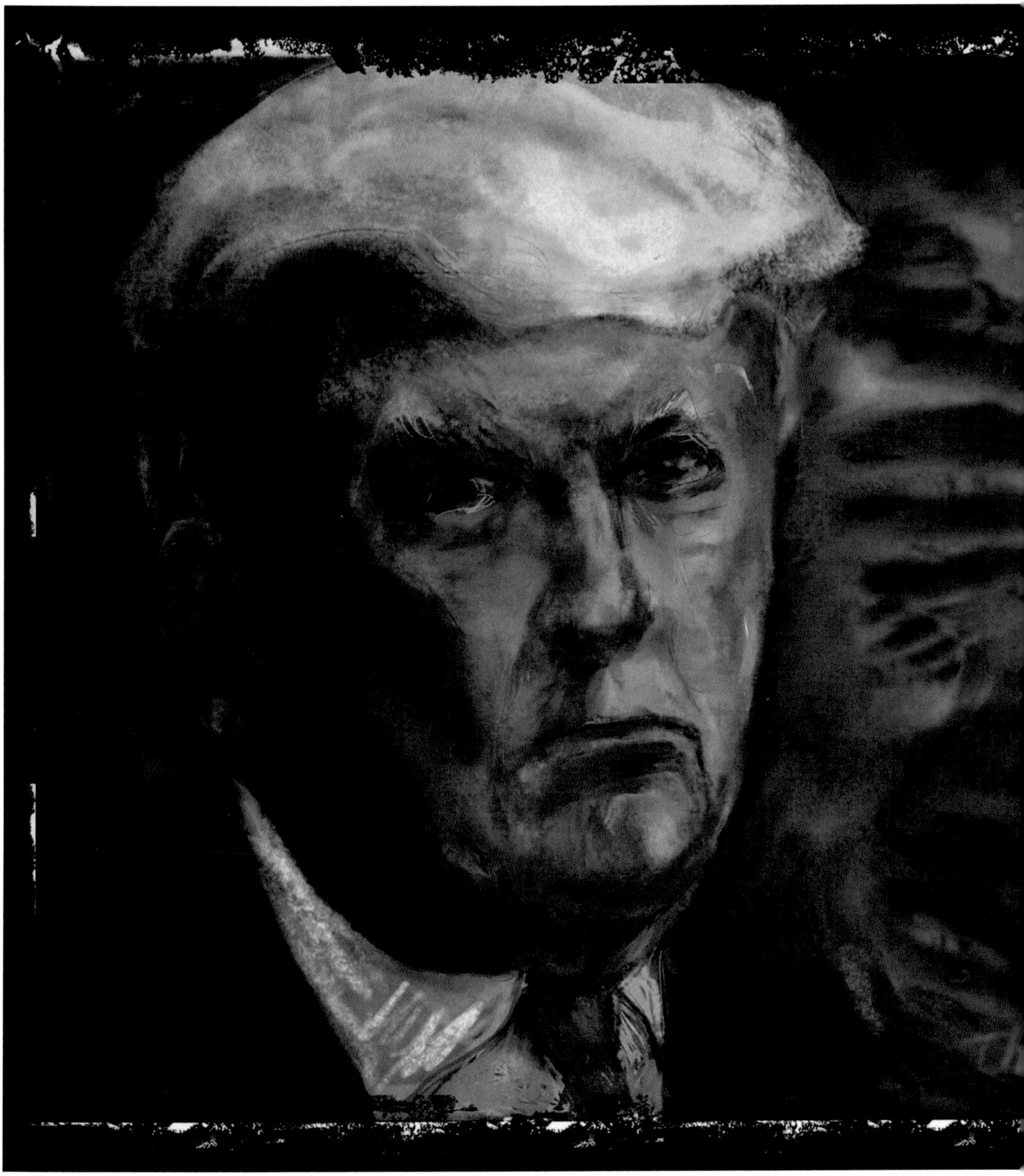

Chosen One

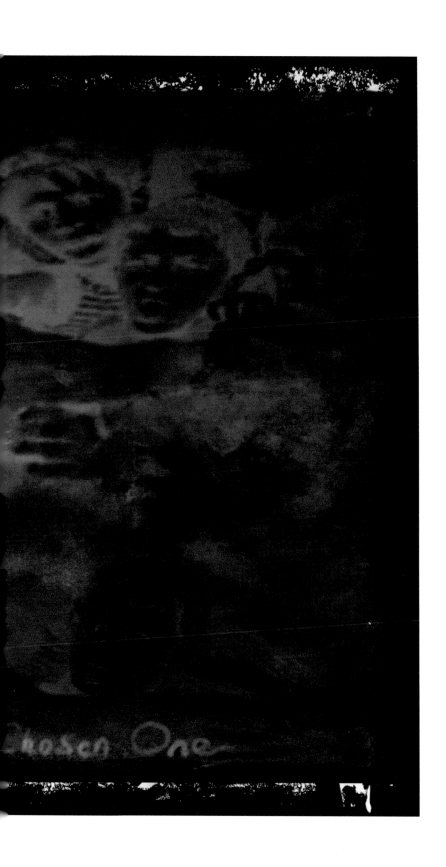

47. **The Chosen One**

PREVIOUS PAGES:

## LATE EPOCHAL STYLE

In this section of *Tales and Familiars*, on the previous page, I present another person you may recognize. I name the portrait of Donald Trump after what he has called himself: *The Chosen One*. Surely 2020 has been a late moment, and therefore a Late *Style* moment, in American culture.

In some works, the frowning Late Style rebuts the smiling kind. Life does not end serenely: "[r]age, rage against the dying of the light." The reason for the artist's raging need not be purely personal. In fact, there can be a cultural and epochal context for a Late Style characterized by dissonance and rupture. What if a folk has suffered an unsettling slide from the self-confidence of a previous era in its history? In the case of my own and the earlier "Greatest" generation, it might go like this: "Aren't we still the American Hero, the one who galloped in on a white horse, bringing military and financial rescue to Europe—troops to conquer Hitler and a Marshall Plan to rebuild? We're not? Wait, were we ever?" Implied in my portrait called *The Chosen One* is an epochal late context. From a soup of shadows, almost drowning, migrants, plague victims, and the persecuted supplicate the American president, stretching out their long arms.

The painting's context is a capitalism gone rogue, lacking the truly free enterprise and the freely choosing labor force it once touted as its pride. Again, as to free, "was it ever?" When capitalism was young, it grew mighty through unapologetic exploitation of colonized natural and human resources. In contemporary times, immigrants inside and outside the American borders are used and abused; slaves have been transformed presto-o change-o into cheap prison labor; the poor, the old, the different have been sacrificed to the recent pandemic. ex-President Trump put his face on a disenchanting era.

I describe here a context for the painting, one which jibes with Adorno's view of a Late Style that is not just personal but epochal. (Robert Spencer explores this in *Late Style and its Discontents*). Unlike Adorno, I posit no particular system to replace capitalism; on the other hand, the present-day United States, at least in 2020, lags sadly behind the other developed countries in taking a hybrid approach, bolstering a competitive capitalism with an ever-stronger safety net and, in the long run, a set of compassionate values.

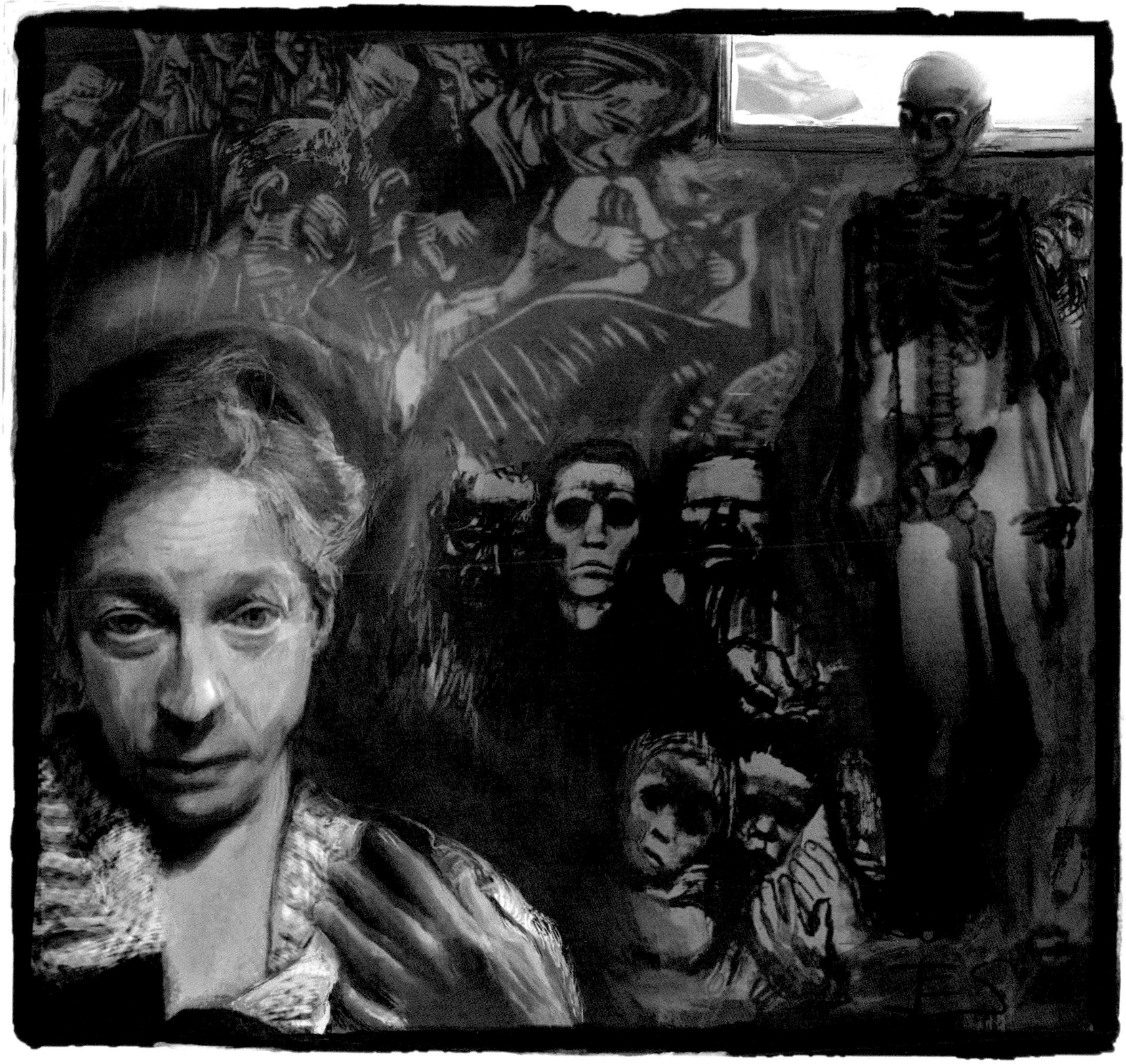

48. **2020—Never Again! (collage w/ Kollwitz faces)**

Prominent in this collage are faces I took from the works of Kathe Kollwitz, a master of empathic art . *Nie Wieder Krieg!* or *Never Again War!* was the title of one of her many political pieces. She lost a son to war and lived through both world wars, persecuted in the second by Hitler. Another reason I appreciate her person and her story is that she considered herself bisexual: "I also believe," she wrote, "that bisexuality is almost a necessary prerequisite for artistic activity, that in any event the element of masculinity in me was helpful in my work." To update, I'd change "the element of masculinity" to "what was once considered masculine." For instance, in this piece I aimed for strength of statement; is that masculine? My approach here is to set 2020, particularly for Americans, inside the ongoing cycle of misery caused by destructive leaders.

FOLLOWING PAGES:

**FAIRY TALES AND LEGENDS**

The good witch Glinda and even the terrible Oz, before manifesting in the flesh, take shape from thin air. In late work, what is the role of a magically-altered universe, as in *The Tempest*? Does it reflect Imagination as, rather than mere fantasy, a True Faculty— one that has its own kind of reality and leaves an imprint on supposedly objective reality? The psychologist Carl Jung asserted that the archetypes in legends and fairy tales dwell in a Collective Unconscious; each person is animated by the Collective Unconscious as much as by his personal consciousness. The archetypes not only crystallize certain natural modes of perception but also shape perception, and, as a result, shape the world. In his later years Jung conceded that era and culture might have some influence regarding the form of an archetype. My own types in the following works have been updated from a woman's point of view. I particularly enjoy portraying intelligence, perspicacity, and dignity in the females. For a change.

## 49.  Beauty and Her Beast

This and the next four works live in the imaginal realm, along with the archetypes and myths. The works update the myths, both by viewing them from a psychological angle and by accenting stature, physical or otherwise, in the women.

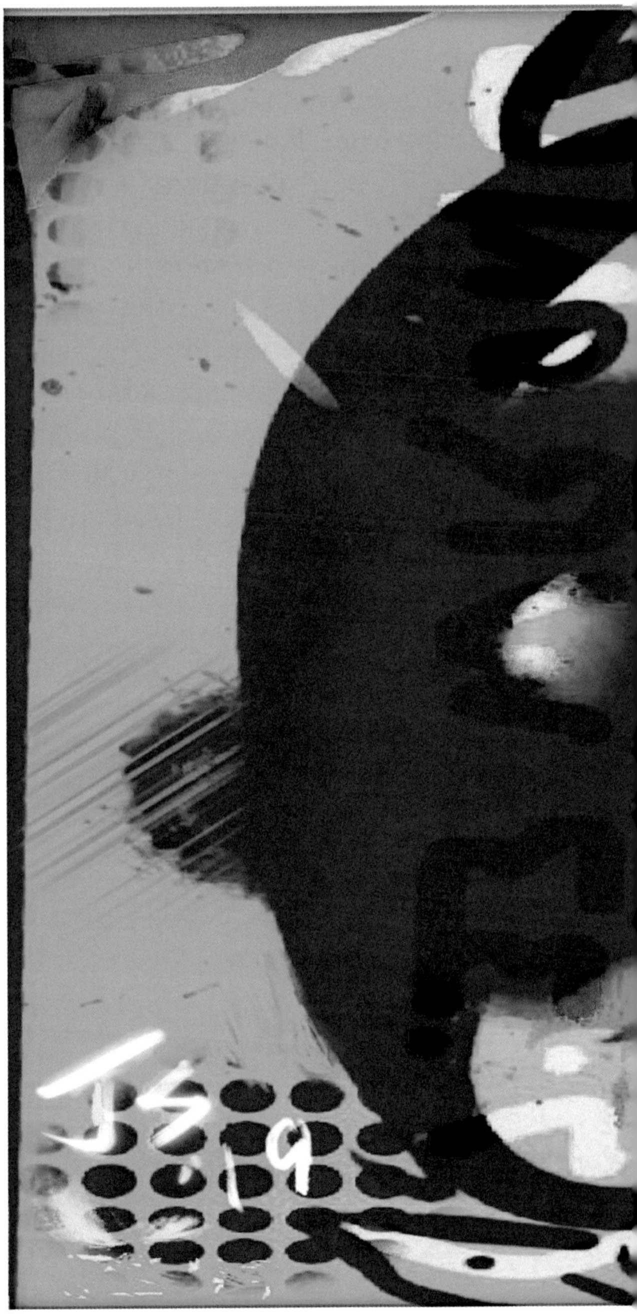

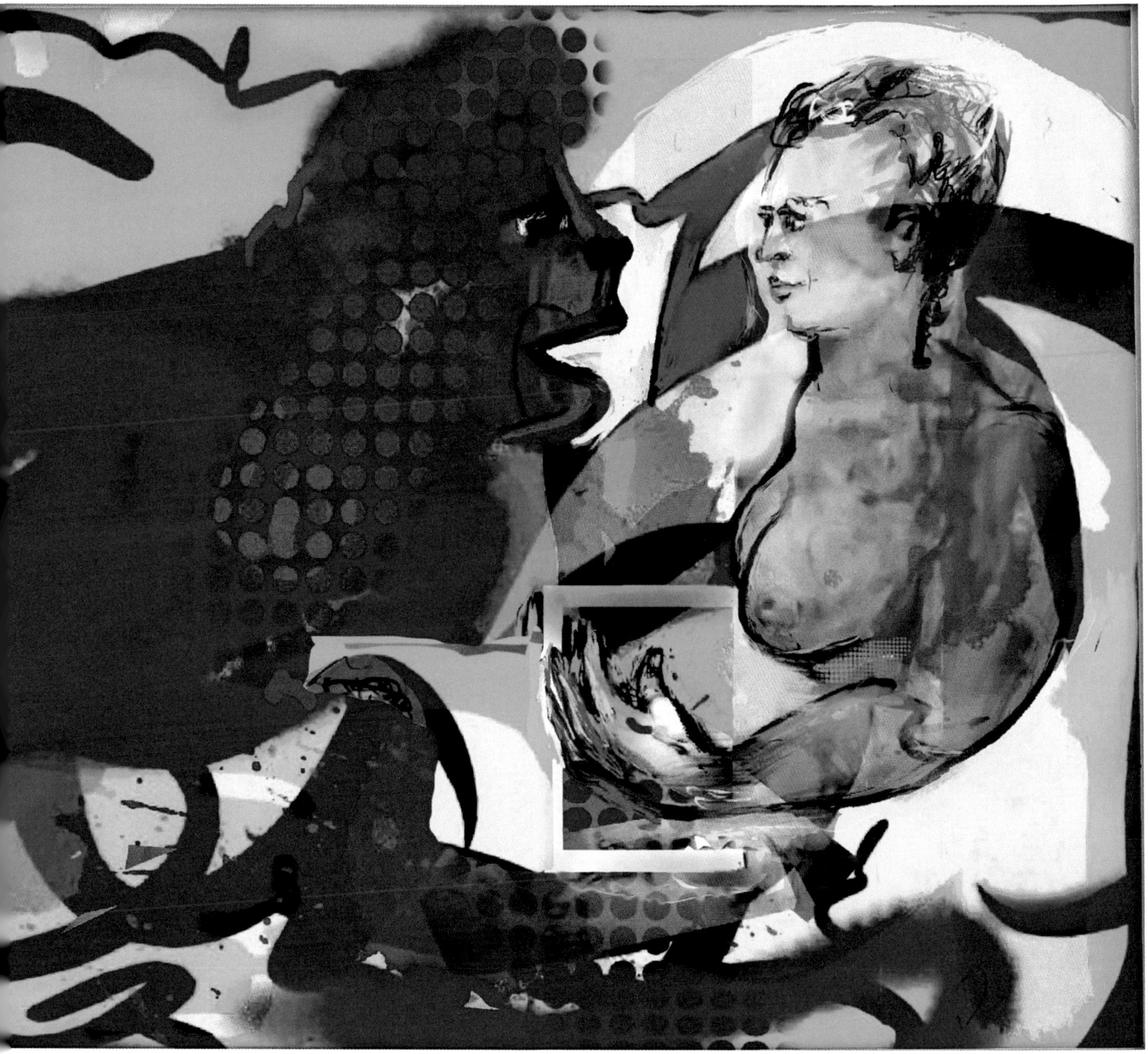

## 50.  **Alice and the Queen of Hearts**

Alice is older here, haunted. Yes there was fallout from her past. "Curiouser and curiouser."

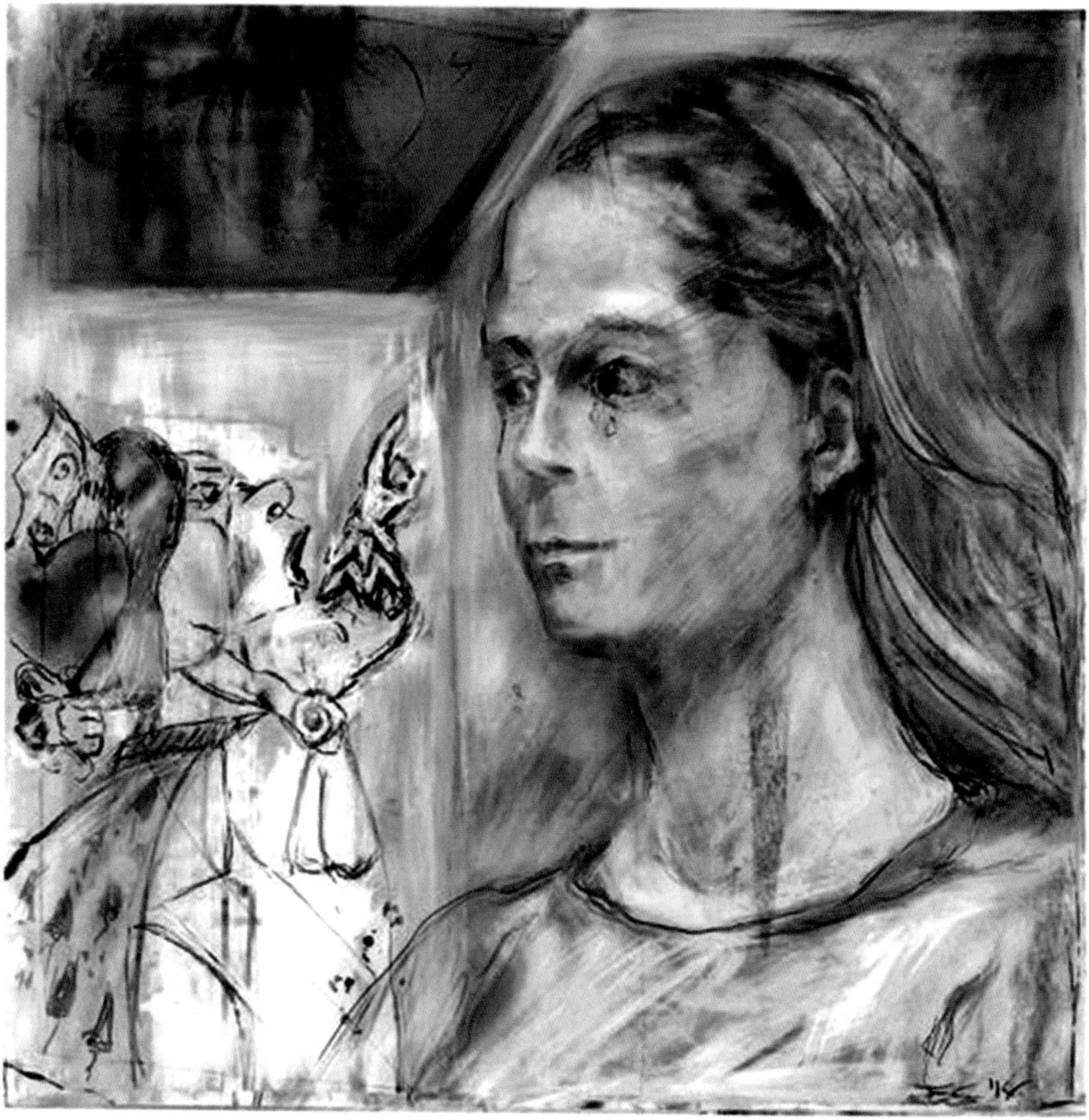

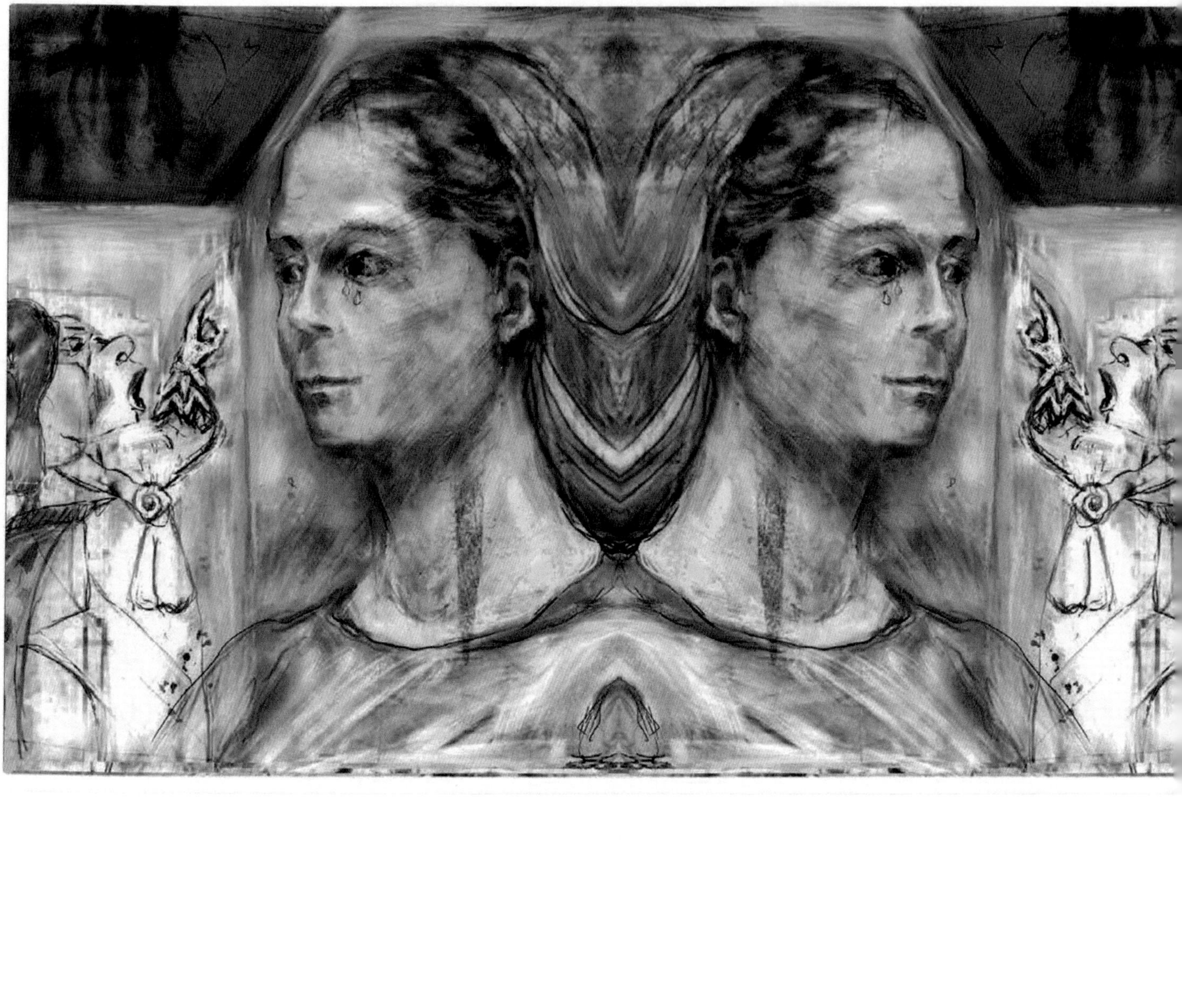

51.  **Alice and the Queen of Hearts IV**

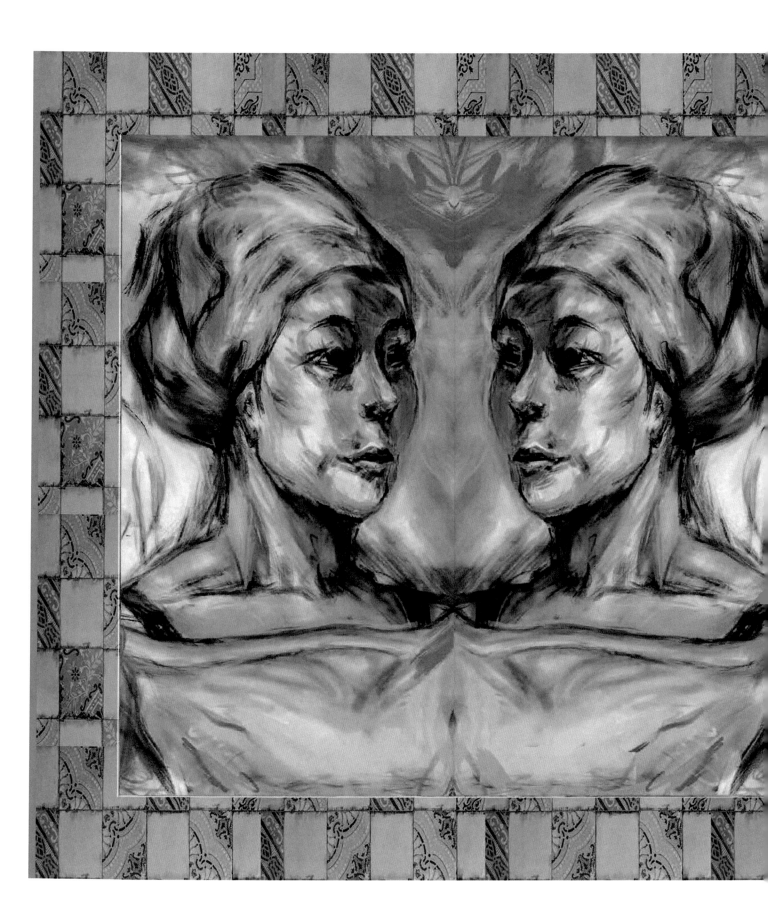

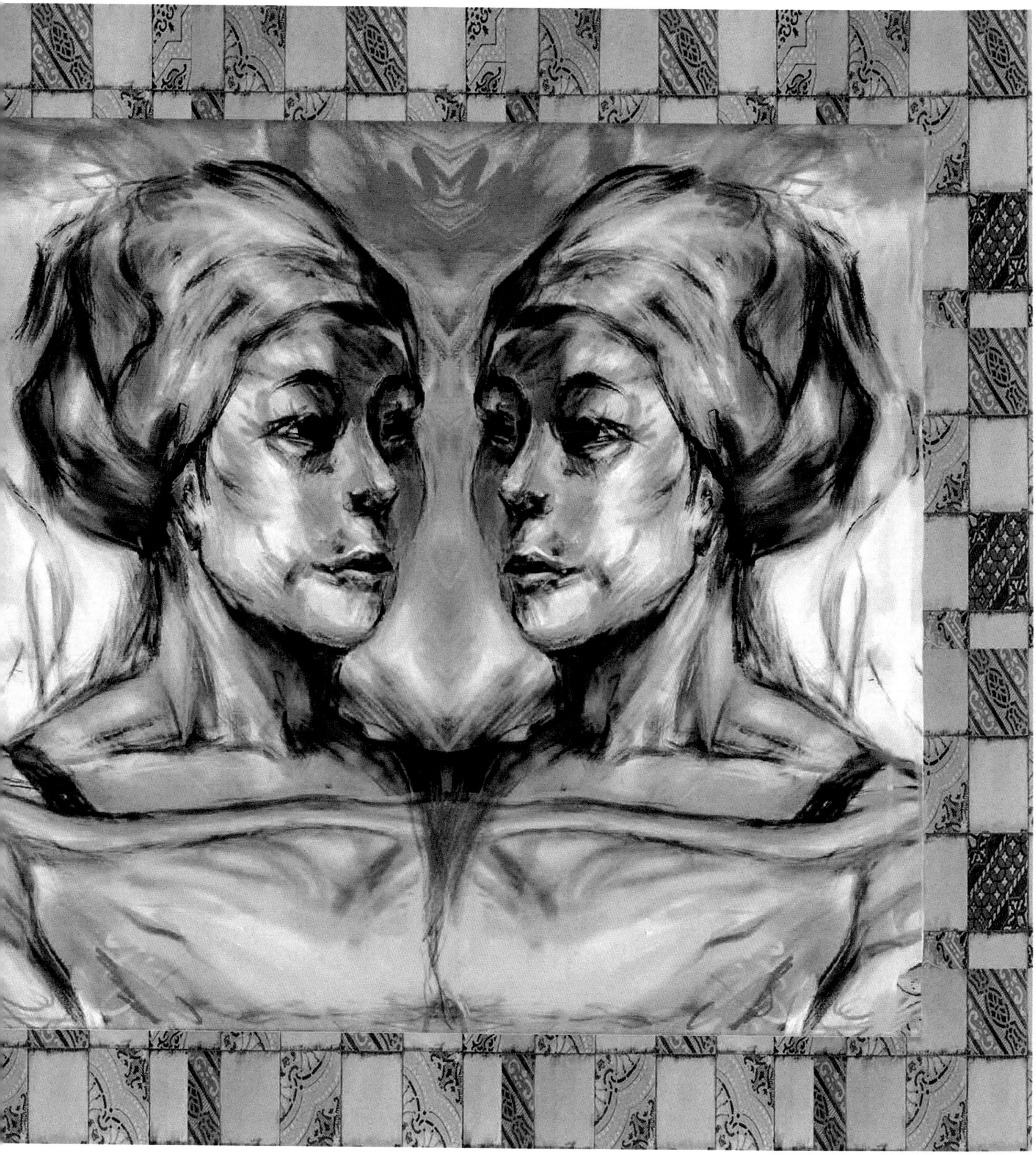

52. **My name is Makani. Makani means the wind.**

53. **Siegmund and Sieglunde** from *The Ring Cycle*. They are twins separated in childhood, tragically destined to meet in later life and fall in love. The story resonates with the painting's dark vortex.

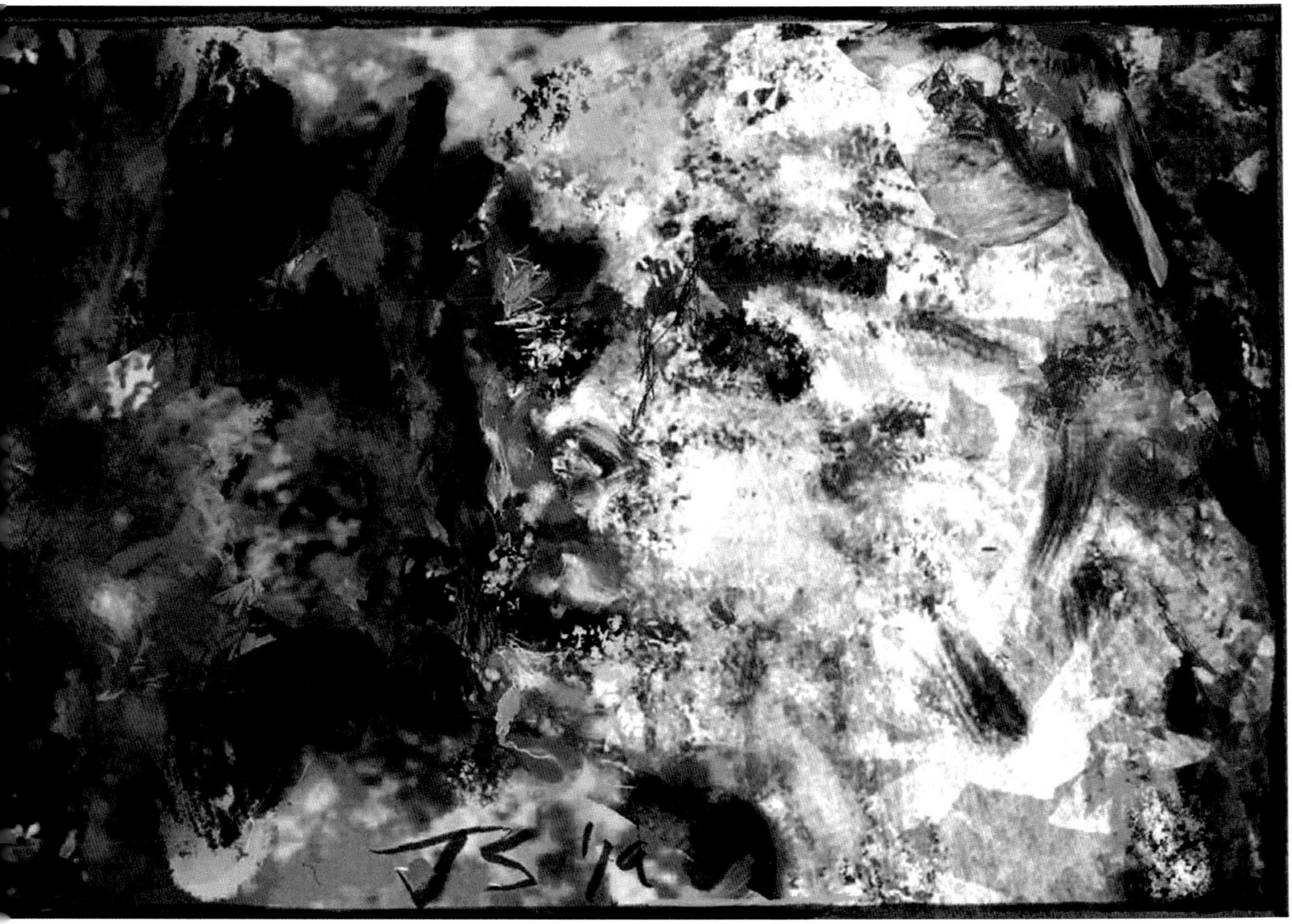
JS '19

In *The Tempest*, Prospero speaks of the "dark backward and abysm of time." Could time have a dark forward abysm as well? My actual painting of these ill-fated twins is printed out as a large banner from an iPad work; the banner is hand-textured with pastel and crusted charcoal.

# TEXTURES

54.  **Self Study at Midnight**

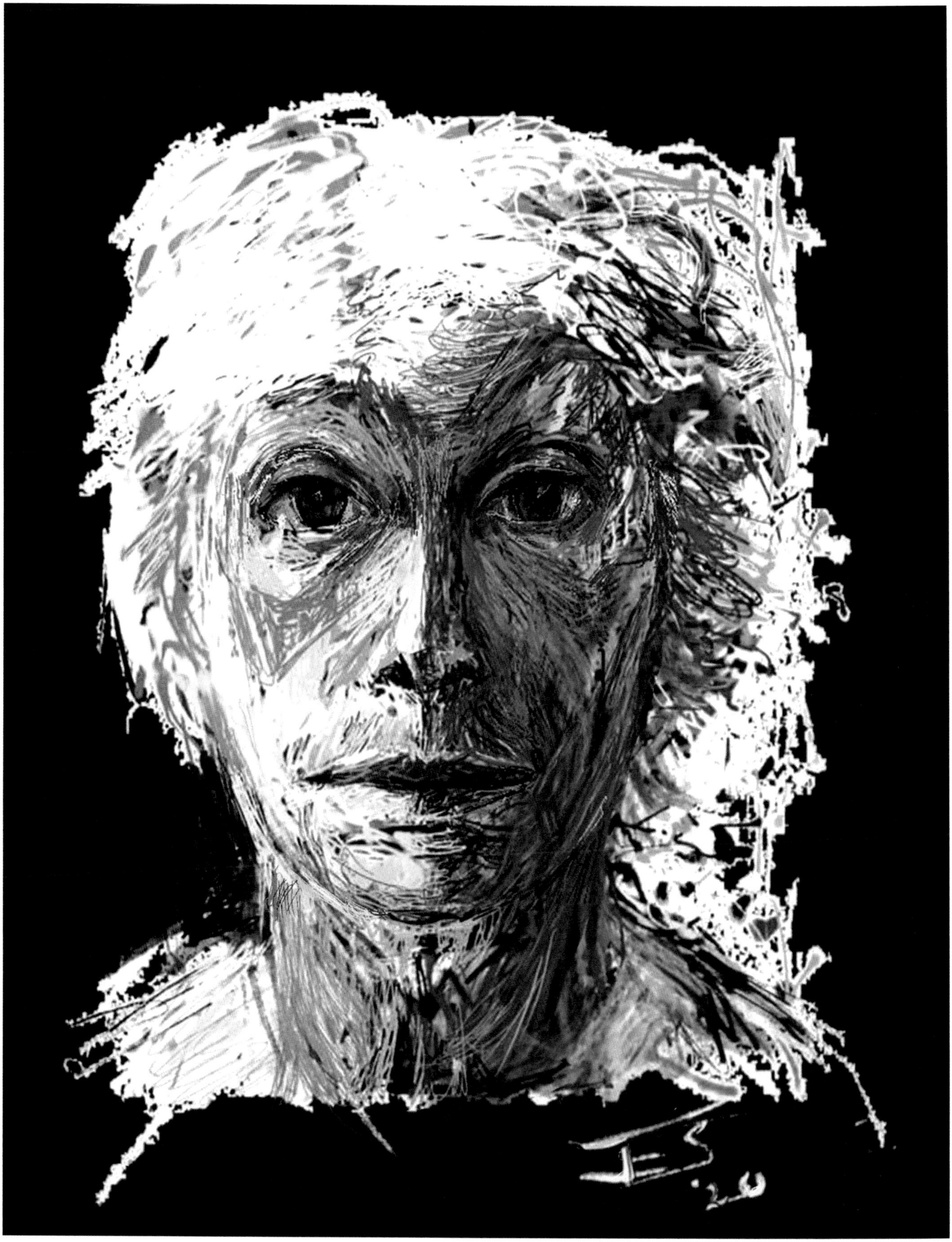

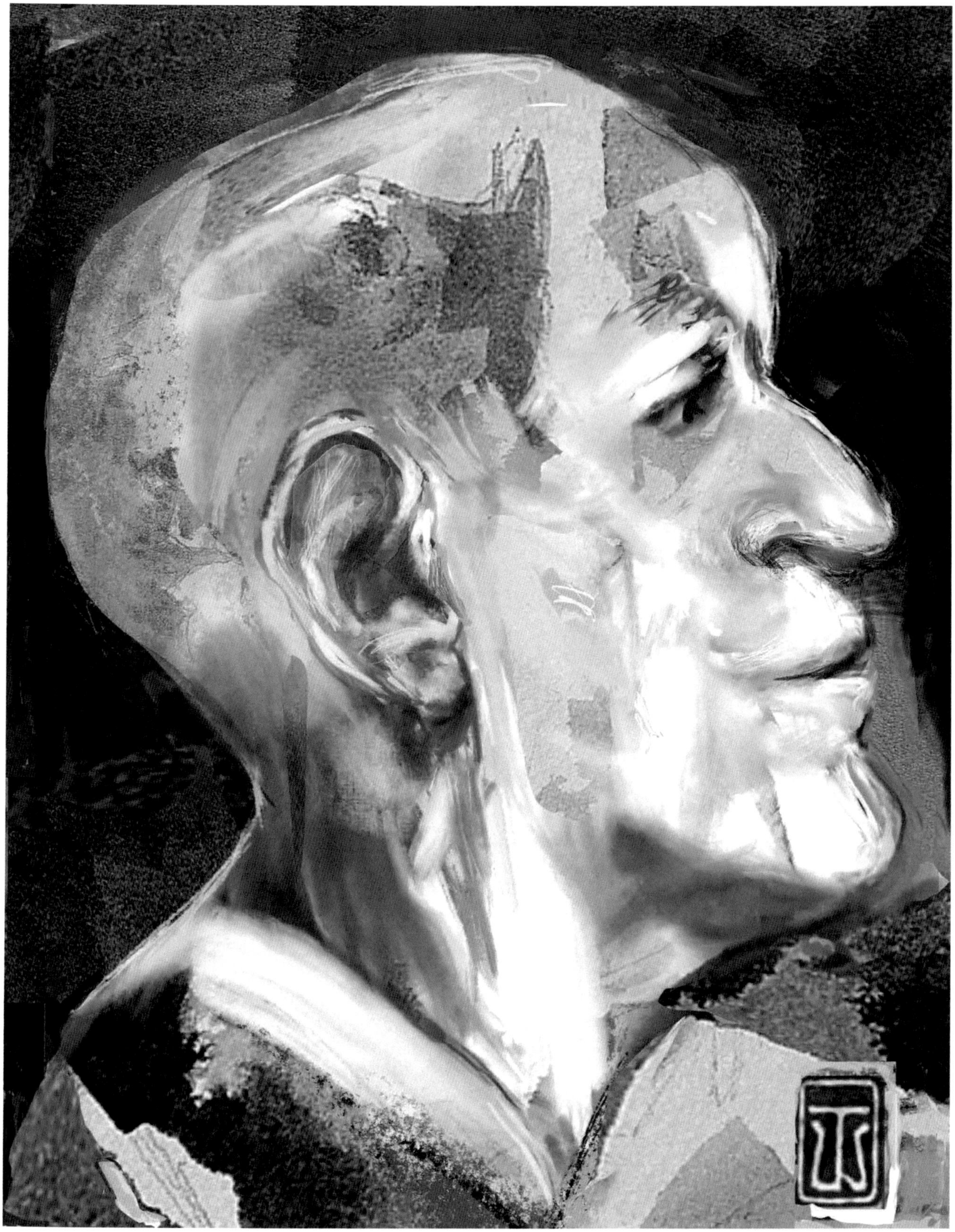

55. **Raymond** He exists in a world of gritty and variegated textures—an urban type, for sure. *Raymond* has an idiosyncratic but unapologetic face. As a model, he displays without shame his aging body. He is who he is, unafraid to stand alone, viewing the world.

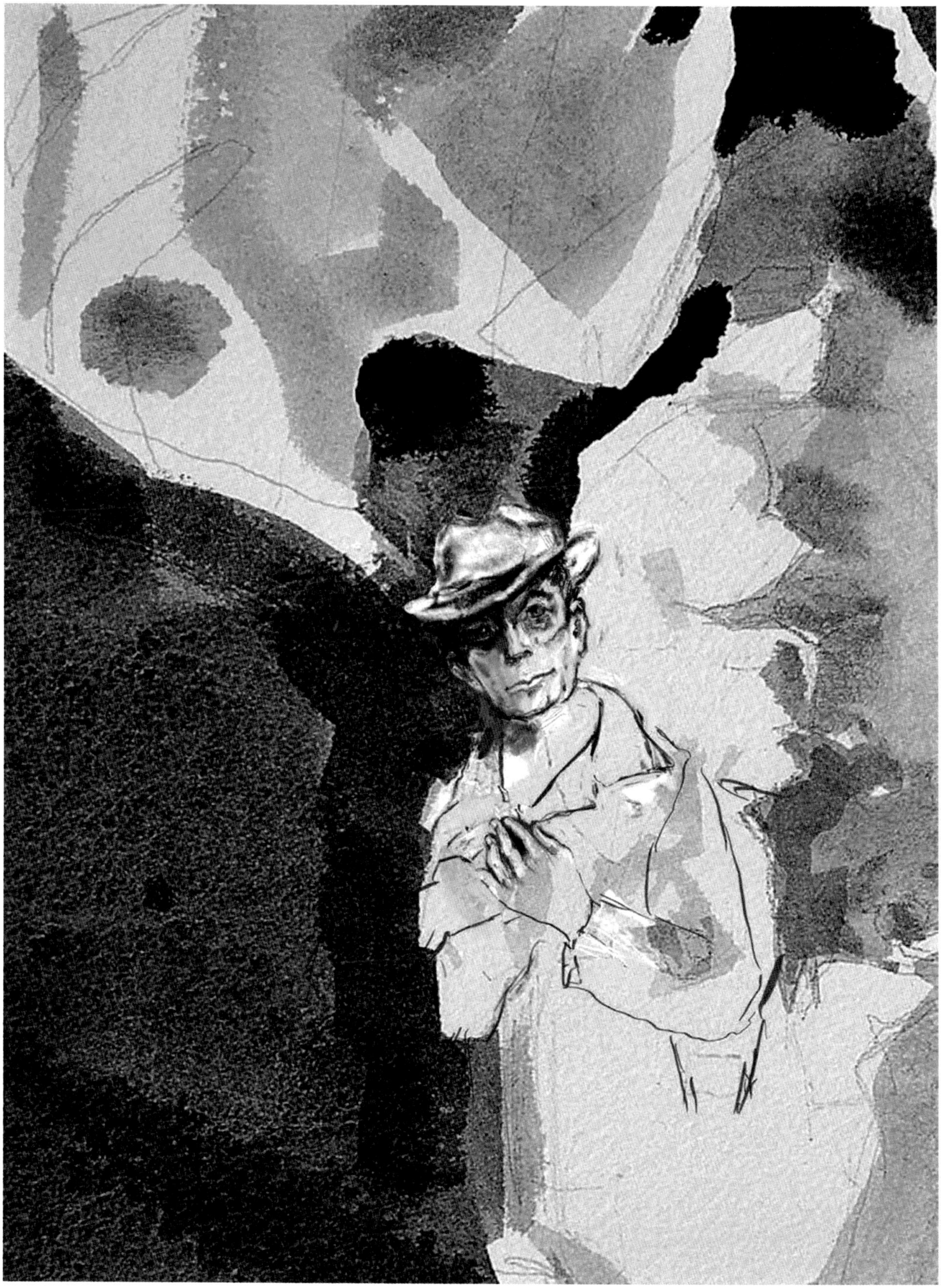

56. **Gumshoe** Here is a *Gumshoe* type, who moves in a world that shadows him against urban cement walls. His job is to pry loose the secret story.

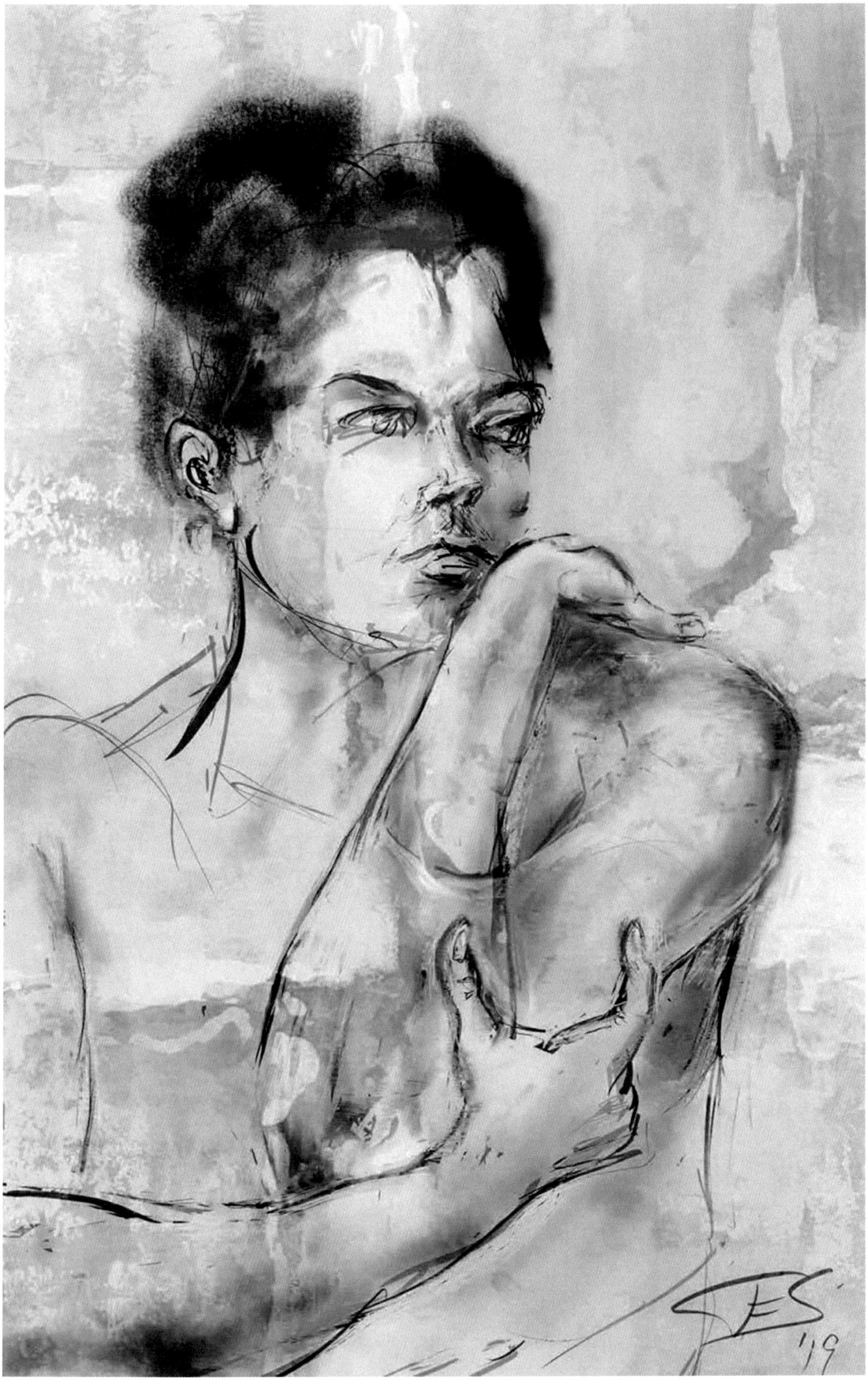

57. **Prudence (**ACROSS). She is a real model, not one of my fantasy figures.

58. **Prudence at her Ease** (ABOVE). She is a single mother, with breasts that have nourished. She's had her men and she belongs now to herself. I'll amend that. She belongs to herself and the son that she adores.

59. **Proud**

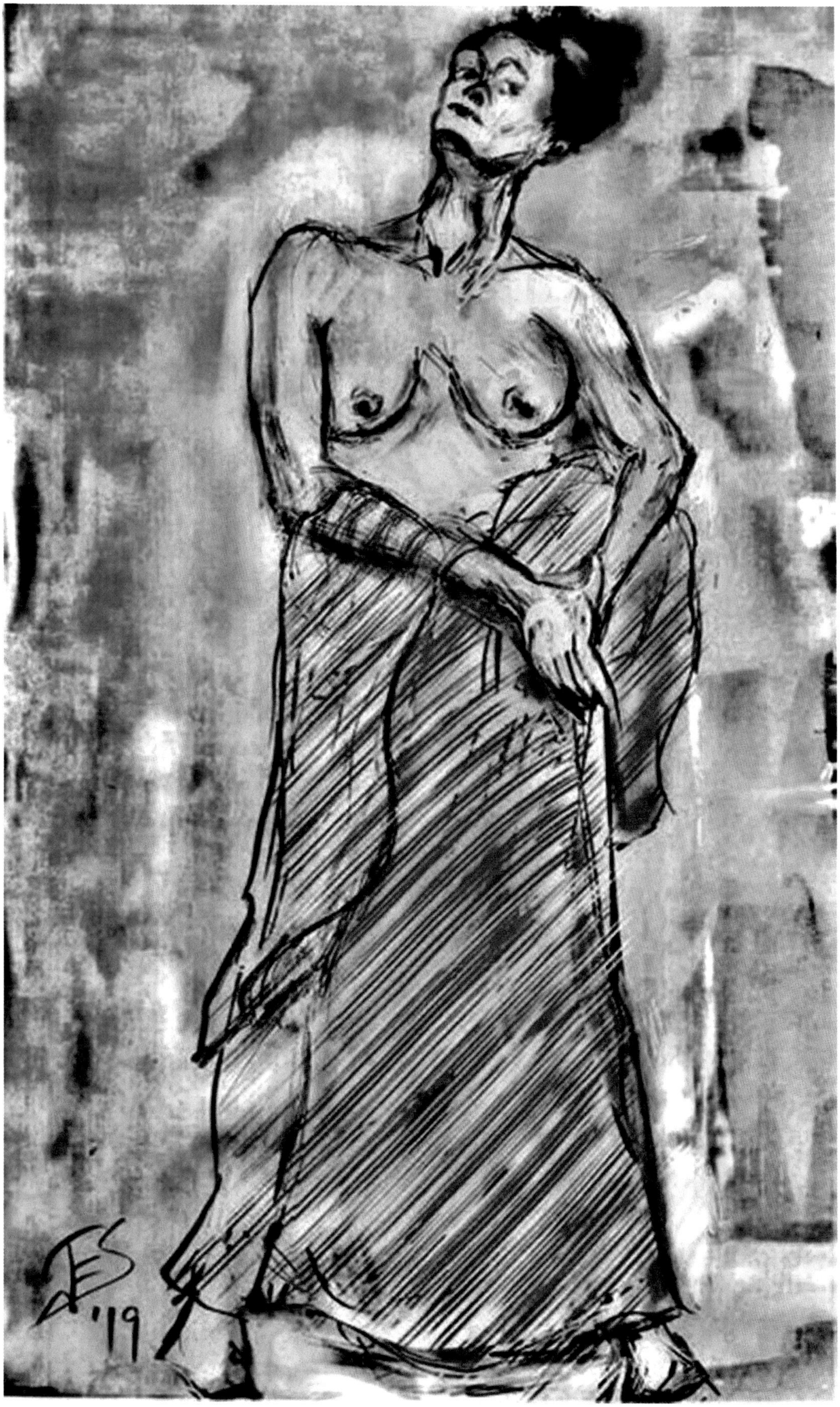
ES
'19

60. **Urban Cowgirl**

This model made her own statement on the stand. She presented as a queer young woman, who had both chosen her identity and built a body to match. The hat was the finishing touch.

61. **Renaissance Man on a Concrete Wall**

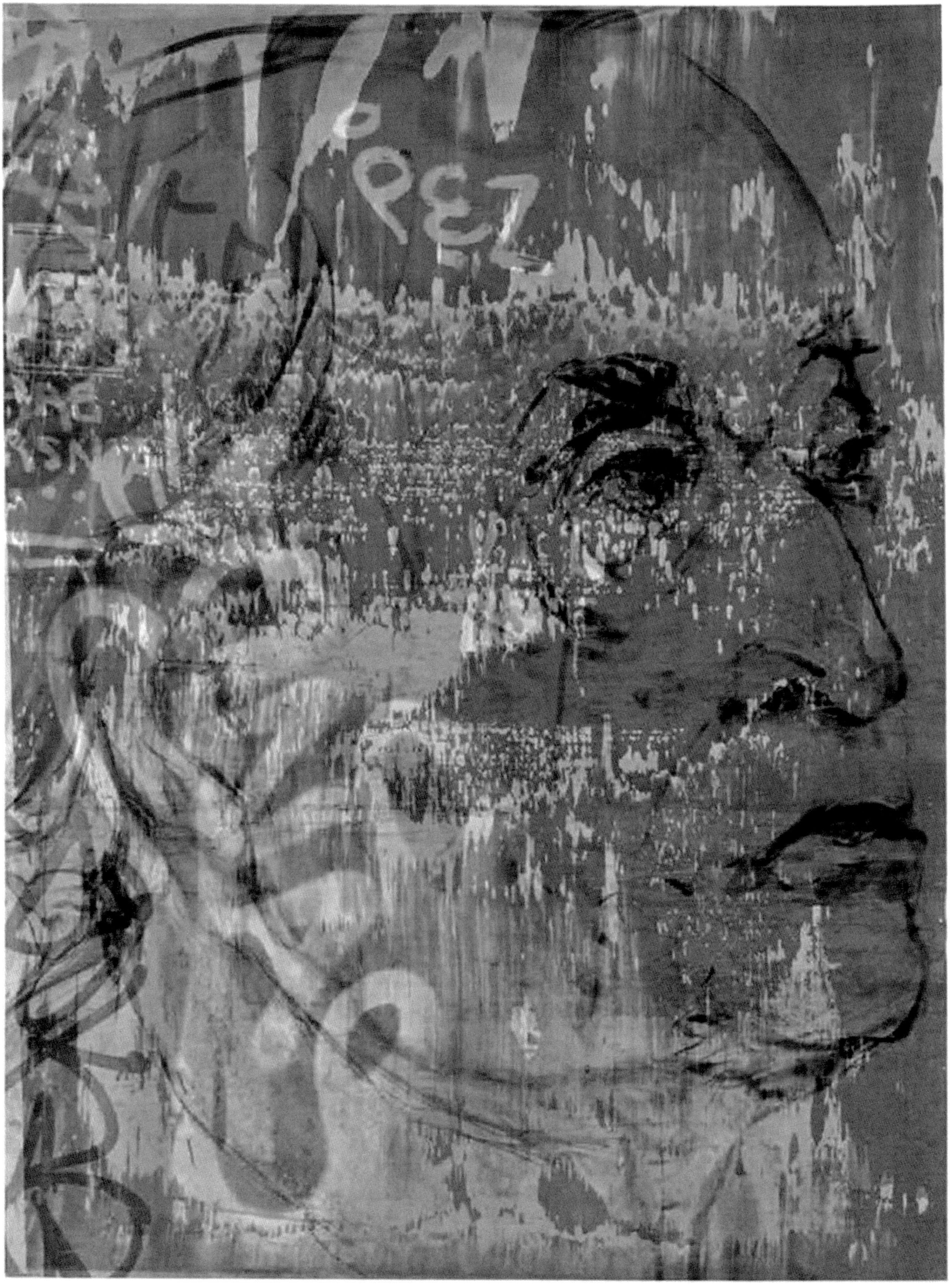

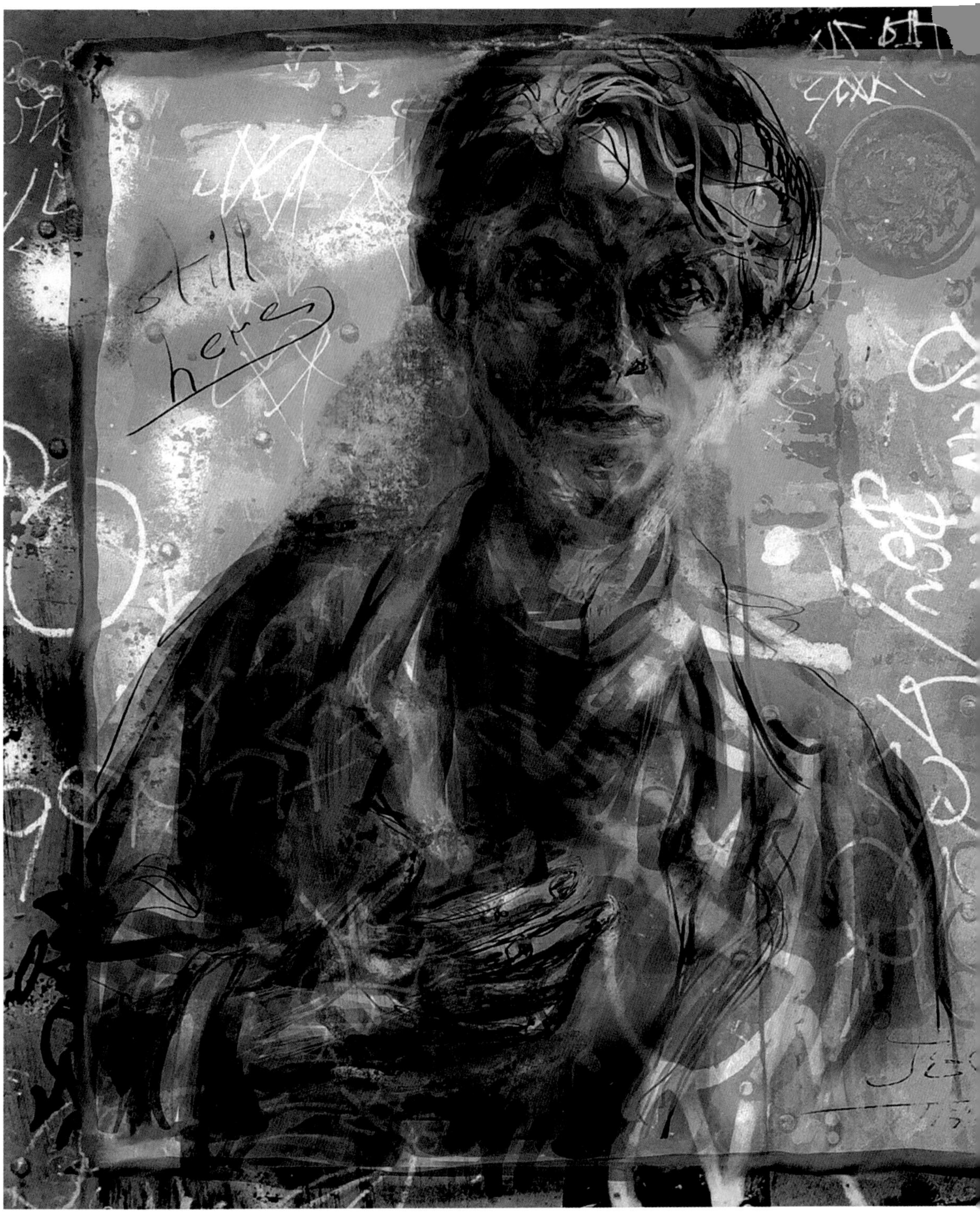
still
here

### 62. **Still Here**

The urban world runs through us,
clutters our consciousness. Still, I'd
rather see aspiring young hoods carry
spraypaint in their hands than guns.

# PATTERNS

## 63.  Yasmine

As I worked this painting,
observing the model, departing
from the model, tattoos entered
into the story. I do not deeply
understand the passion in recent
generations for tattoos. But it is,
after all, to be honored, as an
esthetic impulse at the least. I call
the figure **Yasmine** because she
suggests someone Semitic to me
—say, from Algeria. Perhaps she is
dreaming back on her mother's life
and has still to plan a life for
herself in this new American world.
I enjoy imagining there will be
some kind of art in her future.

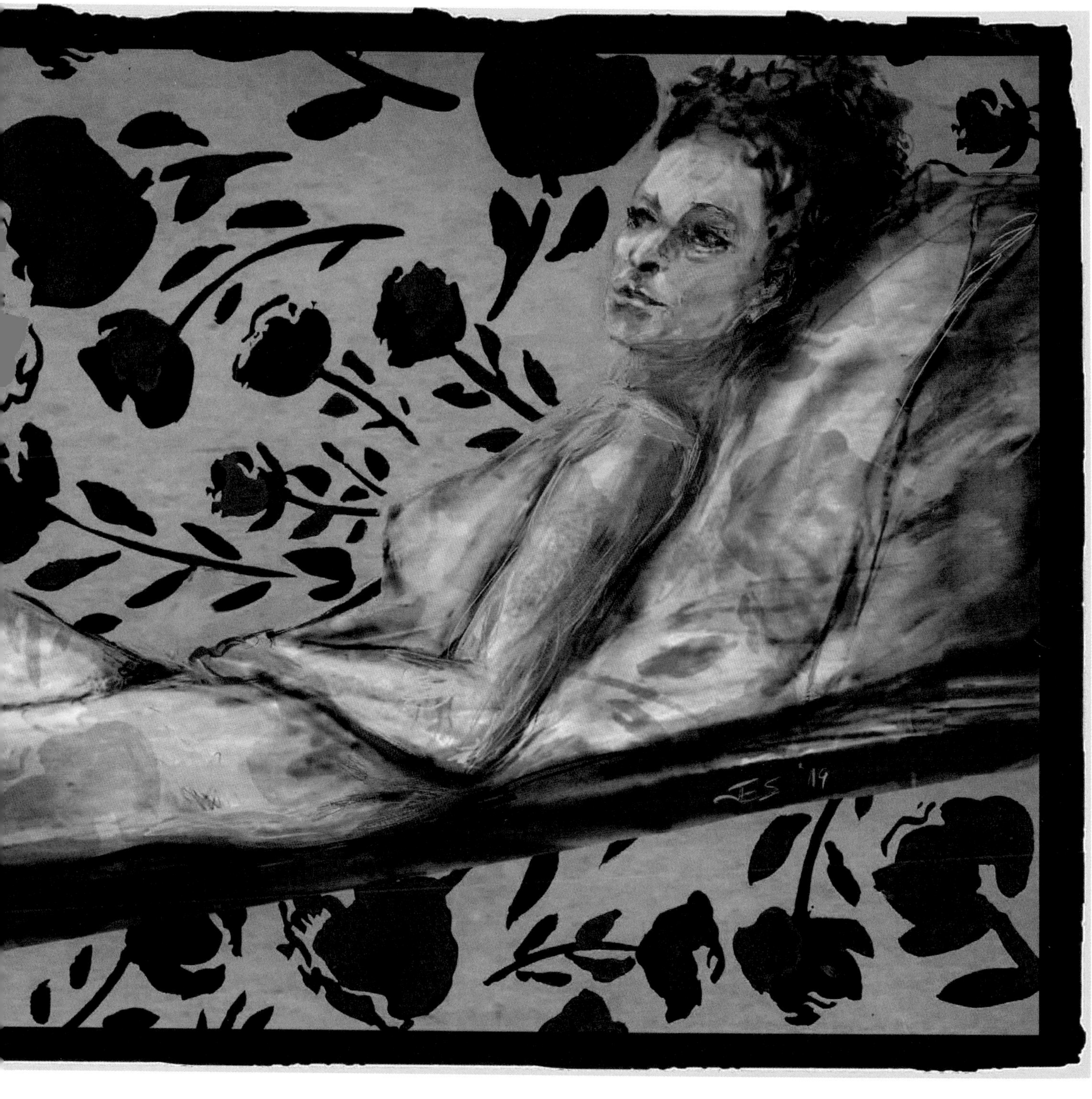

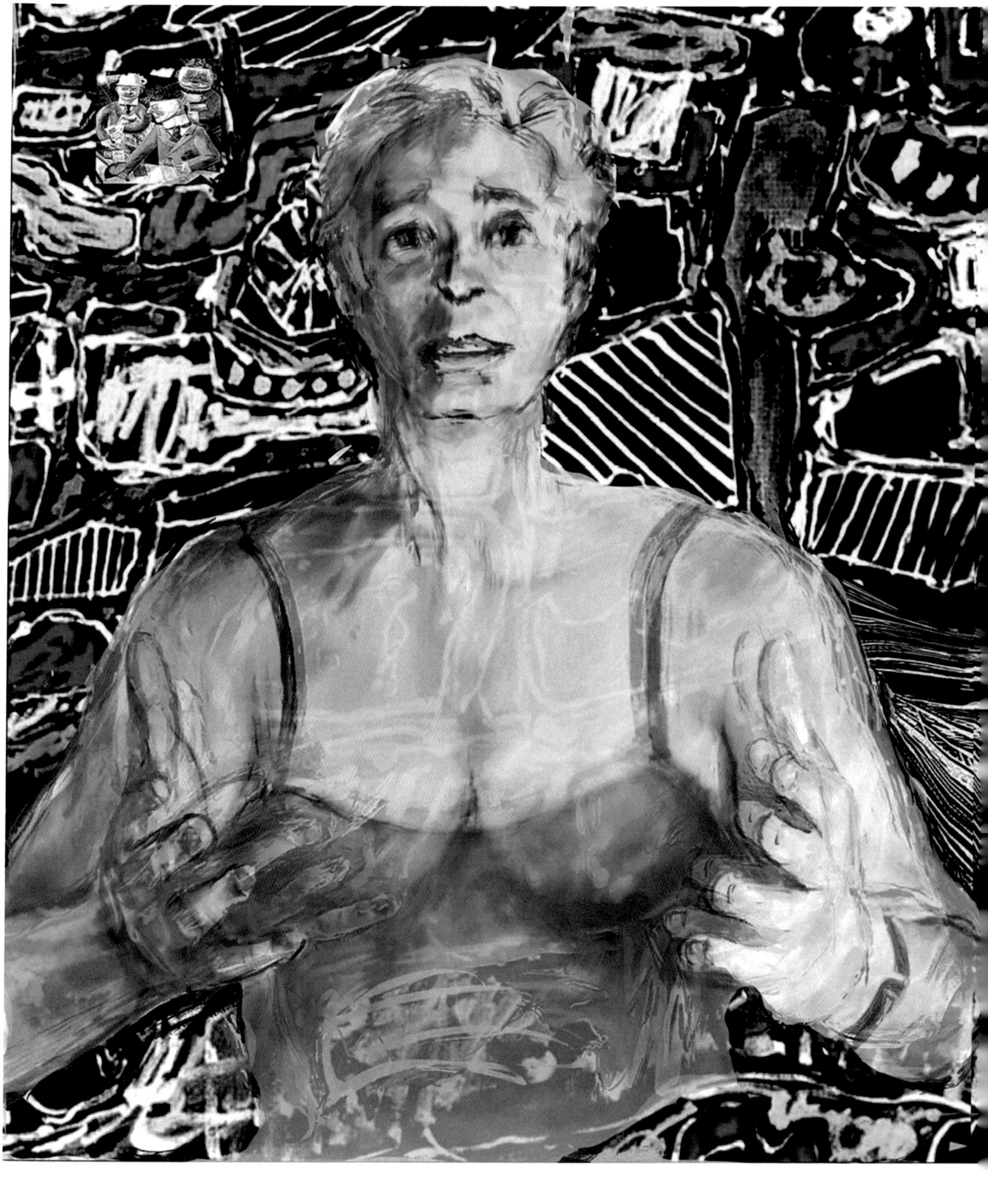

64. **No Mas!** This digital collage/painting, with a nod to Dubuffet, Munch, and Grosz, was done

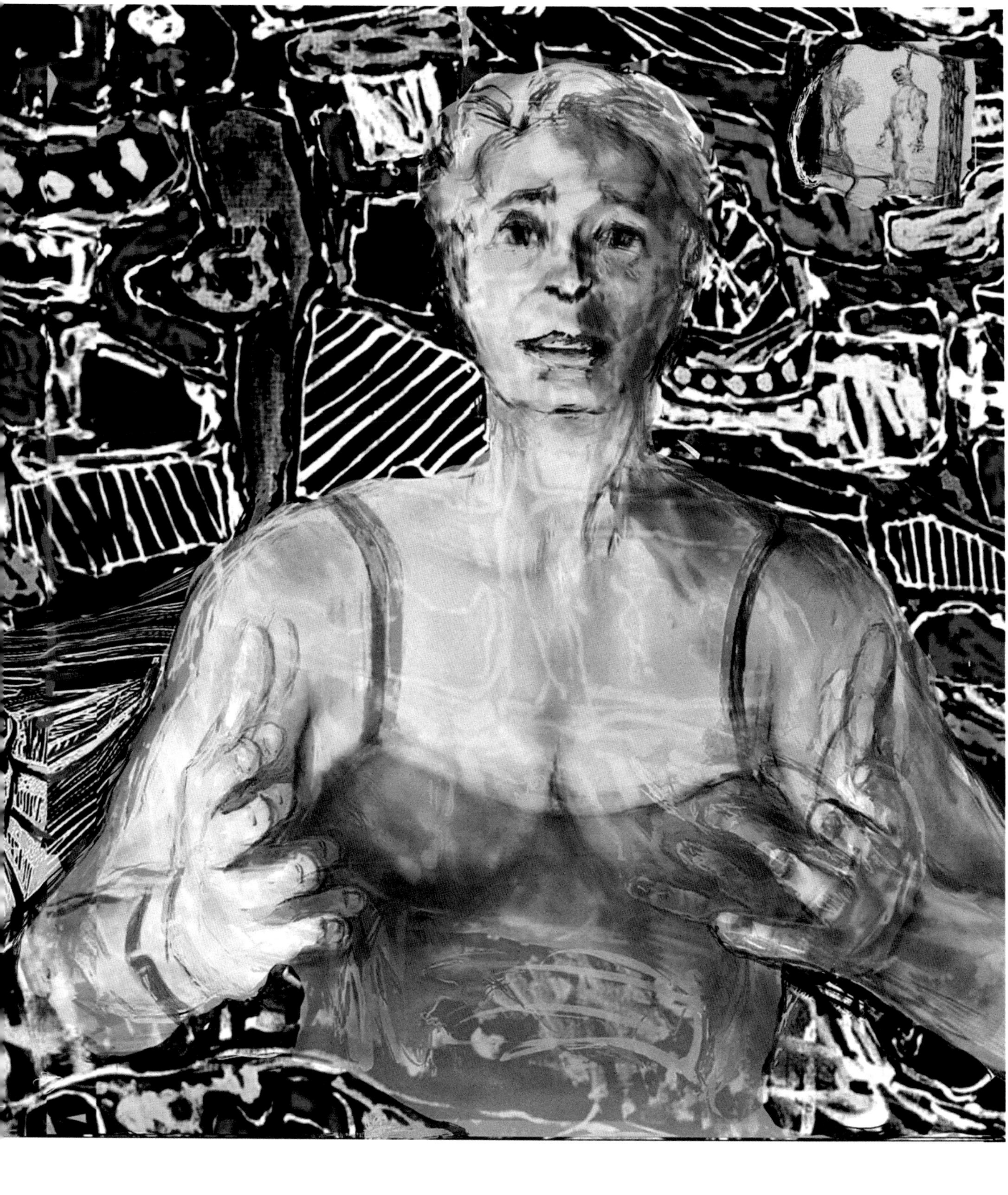

in 2020. It was a year in which global society was in convulsions, both desperate and hopeful.

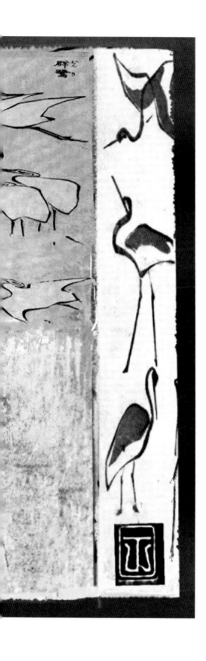

### 65.  **Old Man Mad for Drawing, with Concerned Ancestor**

Here is an homage to Hokusai, the 18th century Japanese artist. He called himself "old man mad for drawing." This interpretive collage gives him a head full of pattern and a life in which realms intersect, Heaven and Earth.

66.     **David**

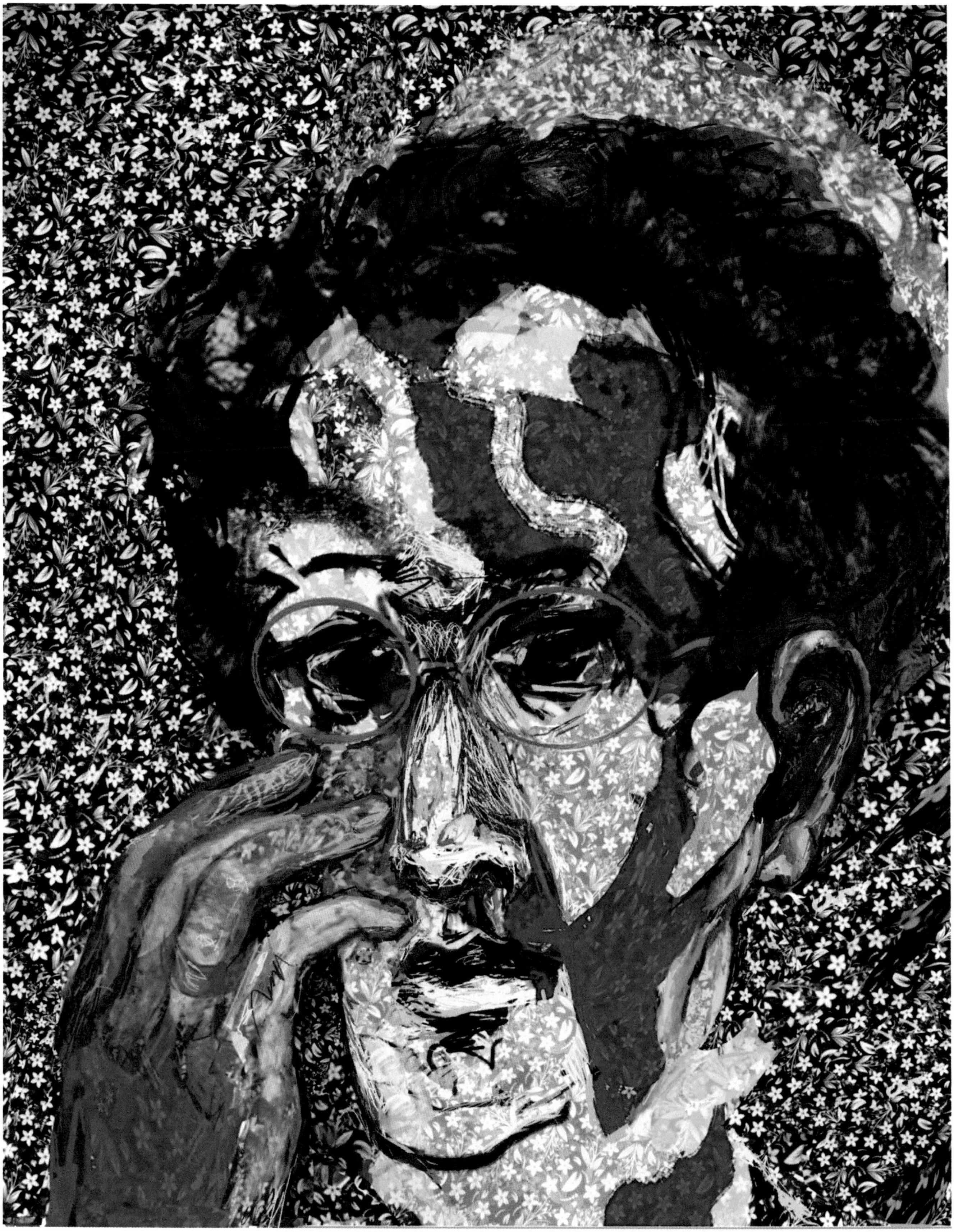

67. **Survivor**

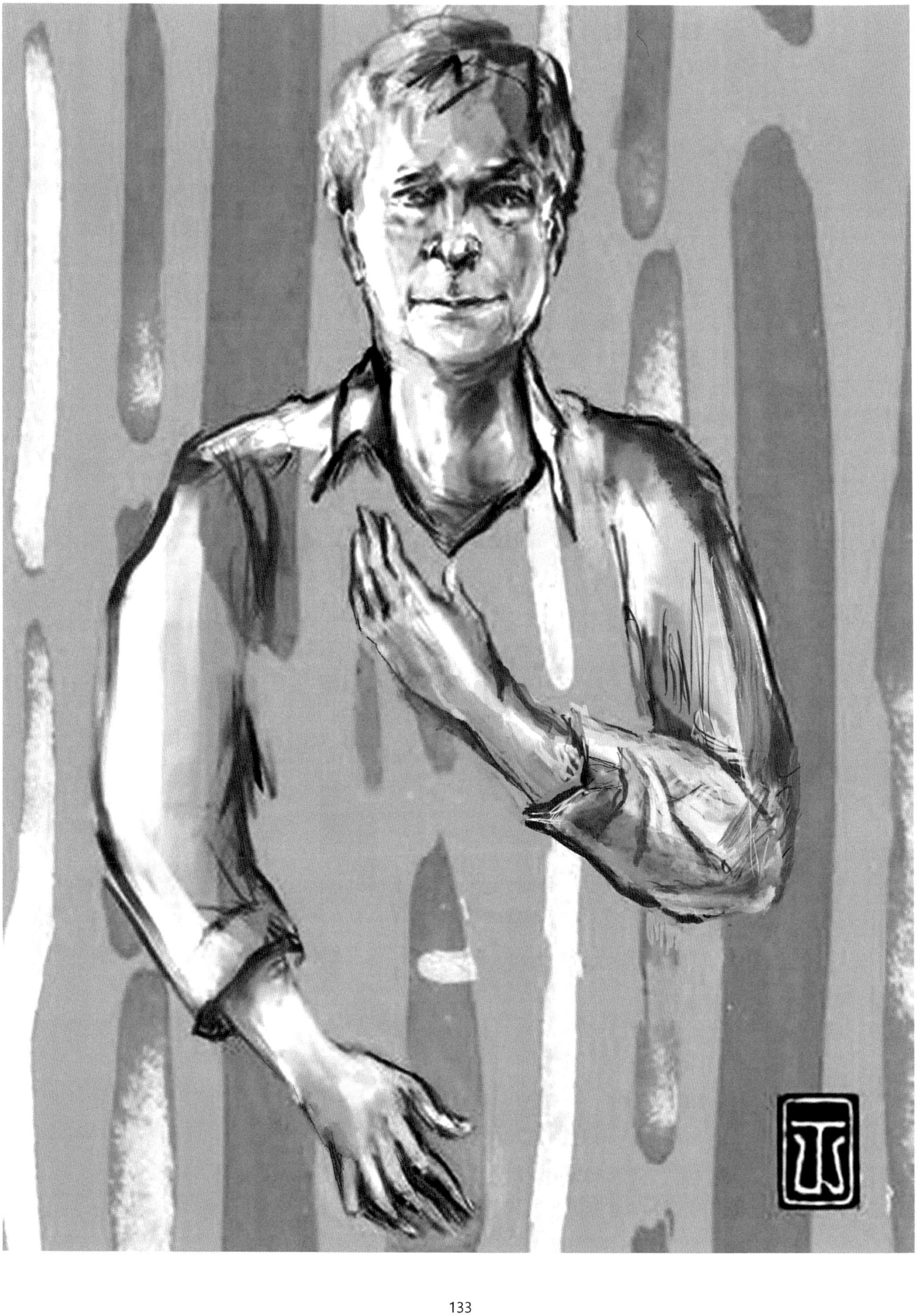

# LIST OF WORKS

1.   **Survivor, Judith**, 2019, scaleable, digital painting
2.   **Brian in Dreadlocks**, 2019, scaleable, digital painting, visual quote from Jasper Johns
3.   **Brian in Dreadlocks II**, 2019, 18"w x 24"h, mixed media , visual quote from Jasper Johns
4.   **Life like leaves falling**, 2018, scaleable, digital painting
5.   **The Witness**, 2019, scaleable, digital painting
6.   **Self-Portrait at Lesvos**, 2019, scaleable, digital painting
7.   **The Refugee**, 2019, scaleable, digital painting
8.   **Grandmother Hope**, 2019, scaleable, digital painting
9.   **Abdullah**, 2019, scaleable, digital painting. This double page includes Abdullah's drawings.
10.  **A Certain Melancholy (Sheltering-in-Place)**, 2020, scaleable, mixed media
11.  **Caring in a Time of Plague**, 2020, scaleable, digital painting, after Goya
12.  **The Artist in Beret and Pajamas**, 2020, scaleable, digital painting
13.  **The Longing**, 2020, scaleable, digital painting
14.  **Reflections**, 2020, scaleable, digital painting
15.  **Torch Singer**, 2019, scaleable, digital painting
16.  **Judith, Post-Chemo**, 2018, scaleable, digital painting from pastel original
17.  **Red**, 2019, 16"w x 20"h, mixed media
18.  **Dancer in Leather**, 2019, scaleable, digital painting
19.  **Lorraine**, 2019, scaleable, digital painting
20.  **IPad Artist, Red Case**, 2020, scaleable, digital painting
21.  **Jemmie**, 2020, scaleable, digital painting
22.  **A Lady Sings the Blues**, 2020, scaleable, digital painting
23.  **The Long Road Home**, 2020, scaleable, digital painting
24.  **Mercutio**, 2020, scaleable, digital painting
25.  **Alex, Arms Crossed (Homage Park)**, 2020, scaleable, digital painting
26.  **Jen, Sculptor (Homage Park)**, 2020, scaleable, digital painting
27.  **Framed Figure**, 2020, scaleable, digital painting
28.  **A Life in Theatre**, 2020, scaleable, digital painting
29.  **There is Often a Way Out**, 2020, scaleable, digital painting
30.  **Bridge into Night,** 2020, scaleable, digital painting
31.  **Boardwalk Memories**, 2020, scaleable, digital painting
32.  **Figure at the Window**, 2020, scaleable, digital painting
33.  **Door Underwater**, 2020, scaleable, digital painting
34.  **Steppin' Out**, 2020, scaleable, digital painting
35.  **Parting**, 2020, scaleable, digital painting

36. **Ancient Lake,** 2020, scaleable, digital painting
37. **My Unconquerable Soul**, 2017, 18"w x 24"h, mixed media on brown paper
38. **Brian in a Red Hoodie**, 2017, 18"w x 24"h, mixed media on textured Asian paper
39. **Teresa with Big Hair**, 2019, scaleable, digital painting with Procreate charcoal tool
40. **Man Looking Up**, 2019, scaleable, ink with digital finishing
41. **Judith as Beethoven**, 2014, scaleable, digital painting
42. **Judith in Sepia**, 2014, scaleable, digital painting
43. **Myself as a Man**, 2020, scaleable, digital painting
44. **Edith in Black & White**, 2020, scaleable, digital painting
45. **Michael Cohen**, 2019, scaleable, digital painting
46. **Rachel Maddow**, 2019, scaleable, digital painting
47. **The Chosen One**, 2019, scaleable, digital painting
48. **2020—Never Again!**, 2020, scaleable, digital painting
49. **Beauty and Her Beast**, 2019, scaleable, digital painting
50. **Alice and the Queen of Hearts**, 2019, scaleable, digital painting
51. **Alice and the Queen of Hearts IV**, 2019, scaleable, digital painting
52. **My name is Makani. Makani means the wind.**, 2019, scaleable, digital painting
53. **Siegmund and Sieglunde**, 2019, 60"w x 19.8"h, mixed media
54. **Self Study at Midnight (collage w/ Kollwitz faces)**, 2020, scaleable, digital
55. **Raymond**, 2019, scaleable, digital painting
56. **Gumshoe**, 2019, scaleable, digital painting
57. **Prudence**, 2019, scaleable, digital painting
58. **Prudence at Her Ease**, 2019, scaleable, digital painting
59. **Proud**, 2019, scaleable, digital painting
60. **Urban Cowgirl**, 2019 scaleable, digital painting
61. **Renaissance Man on a Concrete Wall**, 2019, scaleable, digital painting
62. **Still Here**, 2019, scaleable, digital painting
63. **Yasmine**, 2019, scaleable, digital painting
64. **No Mas!**, 2019, scaleable, digital painting, visual quotes from Dubuffet, Munch, Dix
65. **Old Man Mad for Drawing, with Concerned Ancestor**, 2020, scaleable, digital collage, homage Hokusai
66. **David**, 2020, scaleable, digital painting
67. **Survivor**, 2019, scaleable, digital painting
68. **Over the Rainbow (Selfie as Garland)**, 2020, scaleable, digital painting

# ABOUT

# THE ARTIST

Dr. Judy Schavrien, artist and psychotherapist, is an inveterate experimenter. Her styling morphs from one work to the next and so do the tools she uses. But there is a theme that runs throughout: the fragility, vitality, and weathered complexity of a human being. Among her numerous books of cartoons and paintings, one is called *Shot Awake—A Painter's Memoir*. It explores, through narrative and art, her recovery from a mugging in which she was shot in the face. It was this midlife encounter with death, along with decades of giving treatment, often to intensely challenged patients, that has made her a fearless portrayer of people—fearless of her sitters' fears, inspired by their powers.

As to her media, she draws and paints using a curator's knowledge of the past along with a techie's knowledge of the present. Having worked in oil, pastel, water and print media, she has recently coaxed her iPad to recapitulate the look of traditional genres, from woodcut to watercolor. Rubbing together the old and the new, she makes sparks.

Schavrien has received fifteen awards for her work in the arts, mostly national and international, along with a nomination for Oakland, California's Artist of the Year. Her friend and mentor was the late Harold Rosenberg, art critic for *The New Yorker* and advocate for the Abstract Expressionists. She feels most akin to the figurative painters, Expressionist and Neo-Experessionist, who drew with their nerves unsheathed.

Most recently she served as Artist-in-Residence for the non-profit organization R.E.A.L. (Refugee Education and Learning International), which helps refugees living in the camps on Lesvos, Greece.

LEFT: **Hey Boomer!** photo by Elaine Cohen    68.  **Over the Rainbow (Selfie as Garland)**

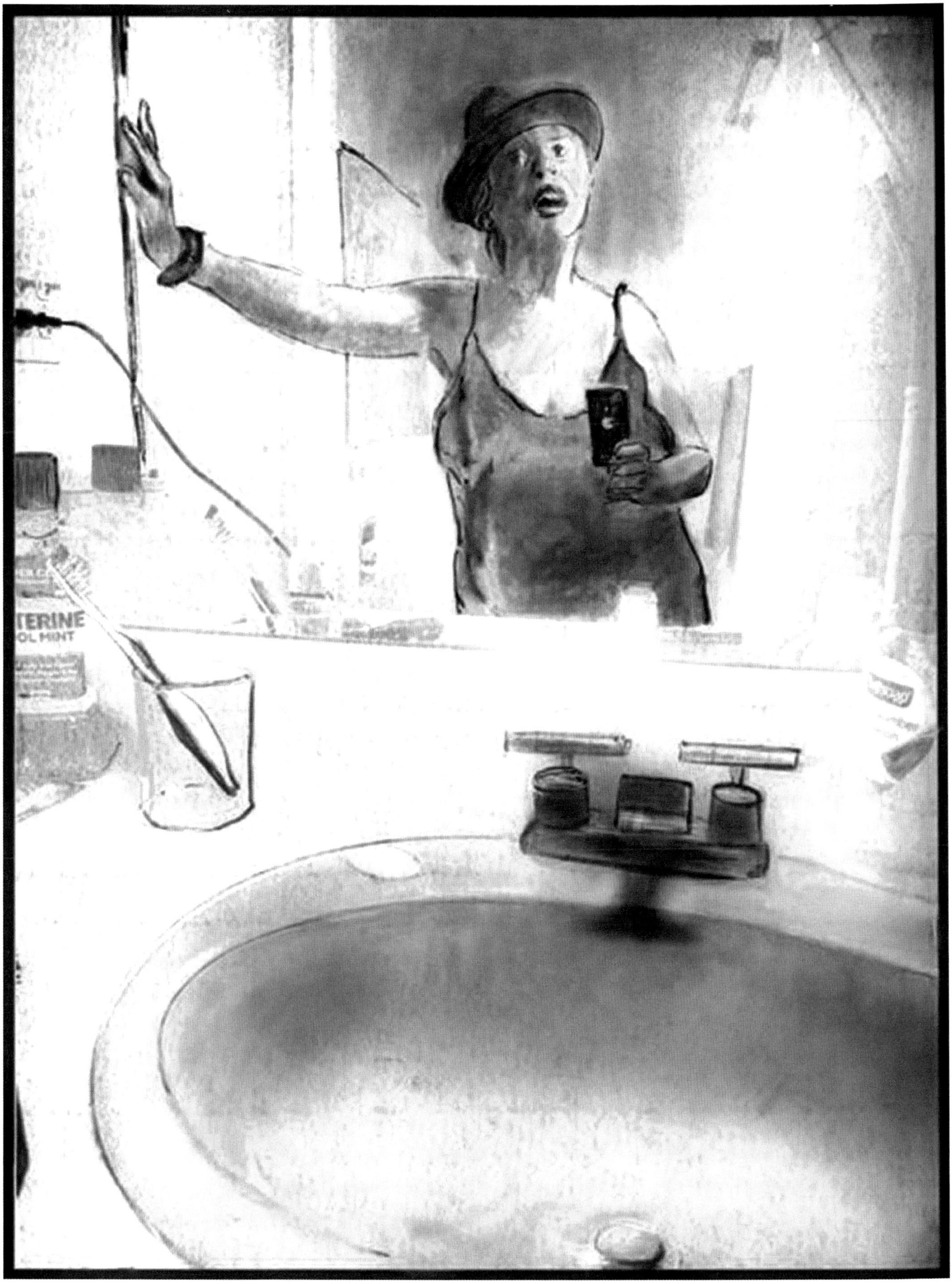
TERINE
OL MINT

# ALSO BY JUDY SCHAVRIEN

## BOOKS

*The New Ancient Greeks: Scroll Paintings by Judy Schavrien*
*Shot Awake—A Painter's Memoir*
*Alice at the Rabbithole Cafe*
*Everything Voluptuous: The Love Songs 1970-2014*
*what rhymes with cancer?* (translated from Harry Brander)

## IN THESE ANTHOLOGIES

*Embracing the Reaper, Journal of Transpersonal Psychology*
*New Lesbian Writing*
*Amazon Allstars: Thirteen Lesbian Plays, with Essays and Commentary*
*Wave: A Confluence of Women's Voices* (web publication featuring
Maxine Hong Kingston) http://aroomofherownfoundation.org/contents/#)

# KUDOS FOR EARLIER WORKS

For *what rhymes with cancer?*

"Harry Brander is a tragic poet who speaks to us wholly in essences, without a superfluous word. From him we hear what we hear within ourselves when we concentrate strictly on life and on death. Judy Schavrien makes these extraordinary poems come to life in English, translating as only one poet can translate another . . ."
Saul Bellow, Nobel Laureate


For *The New Ancient Greeks: Scroll Paintings by Judy Schavrien*

"Judy Schavrien's incisive, often corrosive, always haunting portraits explore the tormented souls of many of the key figures of Greek tragedy. In these searingly beautiful paintings and in her erudite commentary on the plays, Schavrien offers lively political and psychological parallels with our world today. This is a master artist and scholar's urgent call for deeper understanding of our troubled universe."
*Joseph McBride, Film Historian, Professor, Cinema Department at San Francisco State University; biographer of Frank Capra, John Ford and Steven Spielberg*

"Schavrien's resolute, yet unrestrained brushstrokes penetrate deep behind the mask, and viscerally reintroduce each ancient Greek hero as an archetype, whose character presents timeless truths about human nature, interpersonal struggles, and sociopolitical battles. As I journey with each painting, face to face, I understand something new about the marks left by being human, about vanity, jealousy, fear, rage, revenge, rebellion, seduction, sorrow, anguish, loss, but also beauty, courage, loyalty, wonder, and hope."
*Dorit Netzer, PhD, Art Therapist and Research Professor, Hofstra University, NY*

"As a director, I appreciate the gender subversive nature of Schavrien's art. This is a good approach for directing in our times. Strong women, sensitive or 'seeing' men, and sometimes an androgyne face that transcends gender altogether. These portraits, always somehow unexpected, are an inspiration. They call me strongly."
*Bobbi Ausubel, Former Chair, The Boston Conservatory Theater Division*

Made in the USA
Monee, IL
26 February 2021

60559600R00086